The Way Into the Holiest

The Way Into the Holiest

A DEVOTIONAL STUDY
OF THE TABERNACLE
IN THE WILDERNESS

EDWARD W. PATTON

THOMAS NELSON PUBLISHERS
NASHVILLE • CAMDEN • NEW YORK

Published in Nashville, Tennessee, by Thomas Nelson, Inc. and distributed in Canada by Lawson Falle, Ltd., Cambridge, Ontario.

Printed in the United States of America.

Text illustrations by Adrienne Sardella

Library of Congress Cataloging in Publication Data

Patton, Edward W.
  The way into the holiest.

  Includes bibliographical references.
  1. Tabernacle—Typology. I. Title.
BM654.P27 1983   220.6'4   82-22561
ISBN: 0-8407-5833-2

To Margaret,
my dear wife,
whose assistance in research,
preparation of the manuscript,
and loving encouragement
made this writing
possible

About the Author

Edward W. Patton is a retired financial executive who has spent a lifetime in the study of the Bible. Patton attended Temple University in Philadelphia, did graduate work at Northwestern University in Evanston, Illinois, and received his Bible training from the Philadelphia College of the Bible. He and his wife, Margaret, make their home in Newtown Square, Pennsylvania.

Contents

Foreword

The Tabernacle in the Wilderness may rightly be characterized as God's Old Testament "Panorama of Redemption." Yet, I have checked in more than a score of theological works, and I am amazed to witness the conspiracy of silence (what the Germans call, *Todschweigung*, silence of death) on the subject. Neither Calvin nor Watson in his *Institutes of the Christian Religion* treats the subject.

Notable exceptions are the two volumes on *The Typology of Scripture* by Patrick Fairbairn, and the extended treatment by Lewis Sperry Chafer in his valuable *Systematic Theology* (8 vols.). Yet an internationally known radio preacher has said: "No series I have ever prepared has brought greater blessing and appreciation of the glories of Christ than this group on the Tabernacle."

How do we account for this omission? Surely, it is not because of the lack of importance of the study. Many chapters in the Bible are occupied with the significance, description, and ritual of the Tabernacle. There are thirteen chapters in Exodus, eighteen in Leviticus, thirteen in Numbers, two in Deuteronomy, and four in Hebrews—fifty chapters in all. Moreover, how can one understand the argument of the grand Epistle to the Hebrews without it? How does one explain the many allusions in the epistles of the New Testament and the four Gospels to the ritual and importance of the Tabernacle? Its teaching covers symbolically almost the whole range of New Testament truth.

Someone will object that the study, involved as it is in typology, easily becomes fanciful and farfetched. Some writers have been accused of being able to hear grass grow. But the misuse of a truth or practice (witness the Lord's Supper in 1 Cor. 11) is no reason to proscribe the study of that truth, but should motivate to greater diligence in observing the norms and limits of the matter at hand. There have been a number of works in this field earlier in this century, and they have been indeed helpful. In recent decades, however, there has been a noticeable lack in this area. Part of the reason, apart from the extravagances of some writers, has been the disfavor into which devotional books have fallen. But this is not a credit to the perspicuity of our age. Consider the wealth of devotional material in the works of Jeremy Taylor, John Bunyan, Thomas á Kempis, H. A. Ironside, F. B. Meyer, Oswald Chambers, Richard Ellsworth Day, L. B. Cowman, and Charles Haddon Spurgeon.

Mr. Patton has purposed to write a devotional study of the Tabernacle in the Wilderness under a title taken from Hebrews 9:8 (KJV). Throughout his work he has held faithfully to his purpose. Being well versed in the letter and spirit of the Scriptures, he has called upon all portions of the Bible to shed light on the significance of every appointment and feature of the Tabernacle, the visible dwelling-place of the Lord of creation and redemption. His choice of the New American Standard Bible is a happy one and well employed. On purpose he has avoided all technical and involved theological discussions. In our day, when legalism manifests itself in a myriad of ways on every hand, it is refreshing to see his adherence and defense of the great truth of the grace of God in salvation, sanctification, and consummation.

As intimated above, the great danger and pitfall of all works on typology is excessive readings into the text of Scripture and allowing the mind to see parallels where none were intended. Mr. Patton has avoided the Scylla of wooden literalism and the Charybdis of unbridled imagination and fantasy. The controlling principle in his study has been to keep Christ central and draw out the heart of the reader to unstinted adoration of the worthy Lord and Savior, then to implement such adoration with a consistent life to the glory of God.

Admittedly, the furniture of the Tabernacle was not an end in itself. It was constructed, used, and preserved for the purpose of illustrating the *one great sacrifice* of all, the Lord Jesus Christ in the fulness of His redemptive, keeping, and sanctifying work. Thus the sacrifices themselves were, indeed, central.

The work is useful, in our judgment, for the new believer, for the mature Christian who has not made the Tabernacle a subject of study, and also for the experienced child of God who delights to think devotionally on the incomparable Person and work of the Lord of glory. We pray that this work may have a wide and fruitful reading.

CHARLES LEE FEINBERG, TH.D., PH.D.
Dean Emeritus, Talbot Theological Seminary
La Mirada, California

Preface

For many years it has been my joy to spend time in the study of and meditation upon God's Word. In these studies my pathway has led many times to the account of the construction and setting up of the Tabernacle in the Wilderness.

As retirement from an active business career approached, I determined to put the fruits of my study on paper. A kind friend, Dr. William White, discussed this project with me informally and later felt that it should be published.

This is no attempt at a scholarly theological treatise (others have done that competently). But, as the subtitle shows, this is a devotional statement of the blessings that have been mine—and can be the reader's—in these studies. Mature Christians will find their faith expanded and made firm. Younger believers will find here an encouragement to "search the Scriptures" and to uncover the great nuggets of truth to be had.

It is my prayer that all who read these pages will come to a new and deeper knowledge "of our great God and Savior, Christ Jesus" (Titus 2:13).

EDWARD W. PATTON
NEWTOWN SQUARE, PENN.
JULY 1, 1982

CHAPTER ONE

SETTING THE SCENE

The medium *is* the message. So said Marshall McLuhan in his book by the same title. He made the point that the way people get information affects them as much as the information itself.

Jehovah has been using various media as methods of human learning since Eden to bring home His message of love and reconciliation to erring and rebellious mankind. When Adam chose to put his will in opposition to God's, he received an object lesson in the making of coats of skin to cover the sinning man and woman. Adam and Eve learned that blood must be shed to bring reconciliation. In another case, Joseph, Jacob's favored son, was rejected by his brothers, sold into captivity, and exalted to a place of preeminence from which he could save his family. His life story clearly outlines the life and work of our Lord Jesus— rejected of men, delivered to the Romans for crucifixion, but raised by God and exalted at His right hand. The Passover incident, too, touching in all its aspects, is a clear example of God's providing the lamb to be slain and its blood to be sprinkled on the lintels and door posts to ward off the avenging angel of death. When the blood was applied, those within the house were safe. There was death throughout Egypt that night, including the firstborn children of the Egyptians and the substitute lambs in the houses of the Israelites. God used these pictures to foreshadow the Lamb of God who would take away the sin of the world.

Now we turn to another picture, the subject of this book. Looking into the Tabernacle in the Wilderness, we find ourselves face to face with the fact that more space is devoted to a description of its courts, its furniture, and its rituals than any other topic in the whole of Scripture. Fifty chapters in the Old Testament deal with its structure, materials, and use. Almost half of the Epistle to the Hebrews is devoted to the Tabernacle. By contrast, the creation of the earth and its preparation for mankind are disposed of in two chapters.[1] John's vision of the apocalypse requires only twenty-two chapters. Therefore, it is important that we spend some time on this subject, which occupies so large a position in God's Word. The time spent will be repaid by a blessing and a deepening of our walk with the Lord.

There are two descriptions of the Tabernacle in Exodus. The first occurs in chapters 25—31, in which God speaks directly to Moses on the mountain. Then, after a parenthesis in which God deals with an Israelite rebellion (see chapters 32 and 33), the second description involves the actual construction of the Tabernacle (see chapters 34 through 40). In the first, God begins with instructions for the ark of the covenant and the mercy seat, where He said He would dwell. Then He proceeds outward to the court, where the sinning Israelite would come with his lamb or goat to seek reconciliation with an outraged God. The second account begins with the courtyard and moves inward toward the Holiest Place, God's abode. The first description shows us sovereign grace, with God Himself taking the initiative in seeking out the lost. Our Lord Jesus illustrated this act for us in the parable of the Good Samaritan, in which the Samaritan "came to him" to help the needy man where he was (see Luke 10:34). The second account shows how the sinner came to God. He appeared at the gate with the appointed sacrifice, drew aside the curtain gate, and entered, approaching the altar. Thereafter, placing his hands on the head of the substitute and confessing his sins, he slew the animal, saw its life given for him, and watched its body consumed by the fire of the altar.

Those two methods of progression are repeated throughout God's Word. In the Epistle to the Ephesians we see God in the councils of eternity coming to the sinner. In Romans the sinner approaches God.

It is of greatest importance that we realize that the building of the Tabernacle was Jehovah's idea alone. In Exodus 25:8 He clearly states, "Let them construct a sanctuary for Me, that I may dwell among them." The Tabernacle was not Israel's idea, by which *they* could invite Jehovah into their midst, but it was *His* initiative, by means of which *He* purposed to be with His covenant people in a most intimate way. This was pure sovereign grace. The use of the word "dwell" in this verse is most important. Jehovah wished a dwelling where He would become part of the daily life of His people.

The Tabernacle has many names in Scripture:

The Tent of Meeting	Ex. 27:21
The Tabernacle of the Lord	Lev. 17:4
The Tabernacle of the Testimony	Num. 1:50
The Tent of the Testimony	Num. 9:15
The Sanctuary of the Lord	Num. 19:20

The House of God	Judg. 18:31
The Temple of the Lord	1 Sam. 1:9
The Earthly Sanctuary	Heb. 9:1
The place which the Lord your God shall choose . . . to establish His name there for His Dwelling	Deut. 12:5

Before beginning His instructions for the structure, God told Moses to "raise a contribution for Me; from every man whose heart moves him" (Ex. 25:2). The nation that had been in slavery a few short months before responded to the invitation with a deluge of gifts. The list included gold, silver, and bronze; blue, purple, and scarlet material; fine linen, goats' hair, rams' skins dyed red, porpoises' skins; acacia wood, oil for lighting, spices for the anointing oil and for fragrant incense; onyx stones and setting stones for the ephod and for the priest's breastpiece—fifteen items in all. The people had seen no drawing or model; they had only heard Moses's word. This outpouring of gifts reminds us of Jesus' joy and willingness to undertake the task of redemption. His response was, "Behold, I have come (in the roll of the book it is written of Me) to do Thy will, O God" (Heb. 10:7).

Where did a nation used to the taskmaster's whip come upon such an abundance of costly gifts? On the night of the Passover, the people, at Moses's instruction, "had requested from the Egyptians articles of silver and articles of gold, and clothing. . . . Thus, they plundered the Egyptians" (Ex. 12:35,36). This was the fulfillment of promise to Abraham over four hundred years before. God had promised to judge the nation that afflicted them, and that, when they came out, it would be "with many possessions" (Gen. 15:14). We read that the Egyptians were so glad to be rid of the Israelites that they "let them have their request." Riddance at any price was the motive. It is also within reason to suppose that the "plunder" represented back wages. Today we might use the word *reparations*.

We should bear in mind that the Tabernacle—its structure, furniture, and use—is filled with meaning. The teaching for our hearts comes from three different sources: (1) types that are object lessons, certified as types by being so identified elsewhere in Scripture; (2) secondary types that are made up of materials that have great meaning in themselves; and (3) symbols that come from the position or use of various materials or objects.

Metals used in the Tabernacle were gold, silver, and bronze.

Pure gold, in an amount equivalent to 1.65 tons (U.S.), was the most costly metal used. At 1983 prices this would be valued in excess of $20,000,000. It is the leading precious metal of the world. In the Tabernacle it represents a holy, just, and perfect God and sets forth His majesty and glory.

Silver came to 4.65 tons (U.S.) in use, with a current value over $18,000,000. This metal came from ransom or atonement money, one-half shekel required of each man of military age. It was a contribution to insure that there would be no plague among them (see Ex. 30:12). In return, wherever the silver appeared, it was looked upon as "a memorial for the sons of Israel before the Lord, to make atonement for yourselves" (Ex. 30:16). While silver could not atone for sin (that was the sole function of the blood in the sacrifices), its use in the building reminds us of Christ the Reconciler, Savior, Redeemer—the One who atoned for our sins.

Bronze is mentioned some thirty-five times in the Tabernacle. A total of 3.3 tons was used in those places where exceptional strength, heat resistance, or durability was important. Having a melting point of 1,985°F, it was important in the altar where intense heat was present. Where bronze is found in Scripture, it represents judgment. This shows us God's wrath being exercised against the Lamb of God, as He was tested, suffered, and bore away our sins.

Linen, goats' hair, rams' skins and porpoises' skins were used for the hangings and coverings of the Tabernacle.

The linen used was most interesting. Made from Egyptian flax, it was finely woven, brilliantly white, and bore a special name, "byssus". This material was used for garments for royalty and persons of rank and has been found in the tombs of the Pharaohs. Linen in one tomb was found to have 152 threads per inch in the warp and 71 threads per inch in the woof.[2] The fine-twined, white linen reminds us of Jesus, the Son of Man, spotless, pure, and sinless.

Woven into or embroidered on the linen were blue, scarlet, and purple yarns. The blue received its name from the Hebrew word designating a deep blue or violet, and may symbolize the color of the sky. It appeared in the hangings of the gate, the door, and the veil. In the blue we see the heavenly origin of the Son of God. The scarlet was derived from an Eastern insect that infests the holly tree. It was gathered, dried, and ground to a powder that produced a brilliant crimson hue similar to the cochineal red used by the British in their flags and uniforms. Here we see Christ, the Messiah, as the sacrificial lamb in His suffering. The purple, a dark red yarn, was a combination of blue and red but was not produced by so simple a process. A mollusk (the shellfish, murex) secretes the basis of this color from a gland. It was extracted and resulted in a deep red-purple which represents to us Christ in His royal estate as King of Kings and Lord of Lords.

Goats' hair was from the black coat of the Eastern goat. It was spun into thread and then woven into materials forming "the tent", which was the first covering above the Tabernacle curtain. This drab color tells us of Jesus, the faithful and true witness, the prophet of God, simple, and in poverty.

Rams' skins dyed red were sewn together with leather thongs to form the next protective layer of the Tabernacle covering. The ram was the leader of the flock. This was the animal that God provided to Abraham on the mountain as a substitute for Isaac (see Gen. 22:12,13). God is showing us in the covering, as well as with Isaac, Christ our substitute, faithful unto death.

Porpoises' skins formed the final outside covering. This material came from a mammal abundant in the Red Sea and Nile areas. It was used for such durable items as sandals (see Ezek. 16:10). It was unattractive, but its toughness protected the Tabernacle from the weather. It fittingly speaks of one who had "no stately form or majesty that we should look upon Him" (Is. 53:2).

Oil, spices, and precious stones were also prescribed by God.

The oil, obtained by crushing the olives of the land, was used for light and for the anointing of the priests and vessels of worship. Of Christ, our Savior and High Priest, we read, "But the Lord was pleased to crush Him" (Is. 53:10) and "God anointed Him with the Holy Spirit and with power" (Acts 10:38). This anointing oil was restricted to use in the Tabernacle alone. Anyone violating this rule was subject to death. Christ, in His unique perfection, is reflected in this anointing oil, "always [doing] the things that are pleasing to [God]" (John 8:29).

Special spices were used for the incense: stacte, a powder from the hardened drops of the myrrh bush; onycha, which comes from a clam in the deep part of the Red Sea; galbanum, a pungent resin from a species of the ferula, pleasing when mixed with other spices; and frankincense, from the bark of a tree. These spices combined to form the incense used in the Holy Place at the golden altar and within the veil on the Day of Atonement. In the incense we see our Lord as the fragrant perfume of God, bringing joy to the Father's heart.

The precious stone for the ephod was onyx; the stones for the settings for the priest's breastpiece were ruby, topaz, emerald, turquoise, sapphire, diamond, jacinth, agate, amethyst, beryl, onyx, and jasper.

Weights and measurements used in the Tabernacle were the shekel, the bath, and the cubit. The shekel was a recognized standard of weight of uncoined metal, used in financial transactions (see Gen. 23:15,16). The standard shekel weighed about one-fifth ounce (avoirdupois). The progression of values was as follows: 20 gerahs = 1 shekel; 5 shekels = 1 maneh; 60 manehs = 1 talent. The bath was a measure of capacity used in connection with liquids, and equaled about 9.8 gallons (U.S.A.). The cubit, a measure of length used by the Hebrews, was set at the length from the elbow to the tip of the middle finger. This was approximately 17.72 inches. There is also a long cubit mentioned in Ezekiel 40:5 and 43:13 which carried an additional handbreadth and totaled 20.77 inches. The shorter cubit is usually considered applicable to the Tabernacle. In discussing the measurements, we shall use feet and inches, converting the cubit at 18 inches.

A most remarkable feature of the Tabernacle is the precision of the directions given to Moses. He was shown a pattern of the building and its furniture and was further warned, "just so you shall construct it" (Ex. 25:9). Materials were specifically named. Sizes and/or weights were given for the furniture, and directions were present for the draping of the coverings. Colors and designs were listed for the embroidery and weaving of the gate, the door, and the veil. "God is not a God of confusion" (1 Cor. 14:33). This was God's dwelling, to be constructed according to His specifications.

As a further item of careful planning, God committed the execution of the Tabernacle construction to Moses, His prepared construction superintendent. The miraculous preservation of Moses's life, despite Pharaoh's edict that all Hebrew male infants be killed, was the first in a long line of conditionings that God had planned for this man. Having become a son by adoption of an Egyptian princess, he received a princely education. Stephen declared before the Council and his accusers that "Moses was educated in all the learning of the Egyptians, and he was a man of power in words and deeds" (Acts 7:22). Moses's teachers brought him in contact with a civilization unsurpassed by any people at that time. His training was designed to fit him for high office under the government, if not even for the throne of Egypt. He became familiar with court life, associated with princes, and likely was exposed to the grandeur and pomp of Egyptian religious worship. He was schooled in the letters and literary ideas of the time. He witnessed the administration of justice. However, he remembered his origin and believed the promises God had made to his people.

At age forty, he enraged authorities and became a fugitive because of his premature attempt to assume leadership. He fled to Midian in the desert and met Jethro, a priest of Midian. While keeping sheep, he learned the roads of the wilderness, its resources, climate, and the mode of life of the inhabitants. Here God gave ample time for reflection and the learning of lessons in humility.

Following his commissioning at the burning bush, he returned to Egypt and, with Aaron as spokesman, led his people out of Egypt, accompanied by miraculous acts of God. He was now eighty years old, but he had learned of God. God spoke to him "face to face just as a man speaks to his friend" (Ex. 33:11). He had found favor in the sight of God and was now ready to oversee this magnificent construction project.

Along with Moses, God supplied a foreman, Bezalel, the son of Uri, the son of Hur, of the tribe of Judah (see Ex. 31:2). God adds the following comment:

> See, I have called [him] by name. . . . And I have filled him with the Spirit of God in wisdom, in understanding, in knowledge, and in all kinds of craftsmanship, to make artistic designs for work in gold, in silver, and in bronze, and in the cutting of stones for settings, and in the carving of wood, that he may work in all kinds of craftsmanship (Ex. 31:2–5).

What a list of skills for the man appointed by God to carry out the task of executing the design "according to the pattern"! Bezalel's name means "under the shadow or influence of God." Perhaps he had wondered all of his life how he came by such a name. God had chosen him, called him, and filled him with His Spirit for this important task—craftsmanship inspired by the Holy Spirit!

Bezalel's selection should help us to realize that God has His called ones in positions of prominence as well as in positions that attract little or no attention. Surely the Holy Spirit can use us as doctors, engineers, secretaries, and homemakers, but also in tasks unseen or unacclaimed in the eyes of the world. God says, "I have filled you with My Spirit for your work."

In a church I attended some years ago, one elderly lady had found an unusual place of service. She was shy and retiring, rather small of stature and certainly not among the world's wealthy. She came early every Sunday morning and folded the programs to be given to those attending the services that day. It seemed such a small item, but it saved the church the cost of having the programs machine-folded. Perhaps there was prayer with each fold that the one using the program might be blessed and that the pastor would have great liberty in the Spirit that day.

In addition to Bezalel, God said, "And behold, I Myself have appointed with him Oholiab, the son of Ahisamach, of the tribe of Dan" (Ex. 31:6). His name means "father's tent", and he was personally to assist Bezalel in bringing God the Father's tent into existence. As a further encouragement to Moses and to Bezalel and Oholiab, God gave the following gift: "And in the hearts of all who are skillful I have put skill, that they may make all that I have commanded you" (Ex. 31:6). "All who are skillful" were then freemen. As slaves they had used their talents on the palaces, temples, and tombs of the Pharaohs. But that was mere apprenticeship. Now, God would add skill to the skillful to produce the building and its furniture for His dwelling.

God would remind us, by His giving of gifts to these workmen and helpers, of how He builds His church, the body of Christ, today. The Spirit of God prepares and gives to the church,

> some as apostles, and some as prophets, and some as evangelists, and some as pastors and teachers, for the

equipping of the saints for the work of service, to the building up of the body of Christ until we all attain to the unity of the faith, and of the knowledge of the Son of God, to a mature man, to the measure of the stature which belongs to the fulness of Christ (Eph. 4:11–13).

In studying the Tabernacle, we are brought face to face with two propositions. The first is that the Tabernacle was a unique building ordered by God, that He might dwell among His covenant people. This figure of dwelling is used many times throughout the Scriptures. Our Lord Jesus "became flesh, and dwelt [tabernacled] among us" (John 1:14), that He might explain God (John 1:18) and "dwell in [our] hearts through faith" (Eph. 3:17). Second, we should approach the reading of Scripture with reverence and expectation. These things (and others) were "written in earlier times . . . for our instruction, that through perseverance and the encouragement of the Scriptures we might have hope" (Rom. 15:4). In disputing with those of His own people, Jesus said, "You search the Scriptures, because you think that in them you have eternal life; and it is these that bear witness of Me. . . . If you believed Moses, you would believe Me, for he wrote of me" (John 5:39,46). To the discouraged pair on the road to Emmaus, He began "with Moses and with all the prophets, [and] He explained to them the things concerning Himself in all the Scriptures" (Luke 24:27). With these words of encouragement from our Lord Jesus Himself, we move on with our study.

We pointed out earlier that there were two ways of approach to the study of the Tabernacle—God's way, in which He moves from the Holy of Holies out to the sinner, and the sinner's approach, in which he begins at the gate

and moves forward toward a full knowledge and fellowship with God. We shall follow the latter path in this study.
"Let us draw near with a sincere heart in full assurance of
faith" (Heb. 10:22).

CHAPTER TWO

THE OUTER COURT

EXODUS 27:9–19; 38:9–20

Across the vast plain at the foot of Mount Sinai lay the tents of some 2,000,000 Israelites.[1] At a rate of six persons per tent there would be over 330,000 dwellings of a people only recently released from bondage. In addition to the people and their tents, there was a great herd of sheep, goats, and oxen. Some of the poorer members of this host kept a few turtledoves or pigeons.

The total area of this encampment has been estimated at approximately twelve square miles.[2] In the center of the encampment was a large open space measuring 3,500 feet in each direction. It was undoubtedly this open space that was used for the assembling of the congregation or the leaders of the people when Moses had occasion to deliver some special instruction or rebuke (see Lev. 8:3). In the very center of this space stood a structure of modest size occupying an area seventy-five feet by one hundred fifty feet. Its tallest building was fifteen feet high. This was the Tabernacle of God in the Wilderness.

From the edges of the encampment, about all that could be seen was a gray object over which hovered a cloud, signifying God's presence in this structure which He had glorified by saying, "I may dwell among them" (Ex. 25:8). As the Israelite moved down through the maze of tents the rows gradually straightened out so that he began to see the outline of the white fence that marked off the boundaries of the Tabernacle.

The fence was seven and a half feet high and, except for an opening of thirty feet at the eastern end, covered the entire four hundred and fifty feet around the building area. Regardless of the direction of approach, the traveler was forced to make his way to the only gate before gaining entrance.

The fence was held upright by sixty pillars, seven and a half feet tall, made of acacia wood, covered with bronze and spaced seven and a half feet apart. Each pillar was seated firmly in a bronze socket set in the sand and held upright by cords running from the top of the pillar to a bronze pin driven into the ground. Each pillar had a top or capital of silver. Running from one pillar to the next was a bar of silver from which the fence was suspended in loose folds to allow for the winds that would tear to pieces a rigid screen.

The material used as the core of the pillar is not specified. Acacia seems the logical choice since it figures so prominently in the rest of the Tabernacle construction. The acacia tree grew slowly in the desert, drawing water from deep running streams. Our Lord Jesus was spoken of figuratively as the shoot "from the stem of Jesse" (Is. 11:1), "a root out of parched ground" (Is. 53:2), and the "righteous Branch" (Jer. 23:5). The deep roots point to our Lord in His fellowship with His Father: "He went off to the mountain to pray, and He spent the whole night in prayer to God" (Luke 6:12). As He stood at Lazarus's tomb, He "raised His eyes, and said, 'Father, I thank thee that thou heardest Me'" (John 11:41). At the well of Samaria, He said, "I have food to eat that you do not know about" (John 4:32). How deep was that communion with God the Father!

The bronze covering shows us the Lamb as bearing the judgment of God on our behalf (see 2 Cor. 5:21), and the bronze socket emphasizes the fact that our salvation is grounded in judgment. It is past, and we face it no more (see Rom. 8:1). We shall see more lessons about bronze in our next chapter on the bronze altar.

The white linen hangings present to us the holiness of God and the purity of our Lord Jesus. There was no one who brought any charge against our Lord Jesus. "Which one of you convicts Me of sin?" (John 8:46), was the challenge of our Lord. "I find no guilt in Him" (John 18:38), was Pilate's judgment. The writer to the Hebrews puts it this way: "We . . . have such a high priest, holy, innocent, undefiled, separated from sinners" (Heb. 7:26).

It is interesting that all of the materials involved in the outer court, save one, came from those who gave as their heart moved them (see Ex. 25:2). The one exception is the silver which came from the redemption money required of every male of military age. These military men were promised a memorial in the Tabernacle (see Ex. 30:16), and here is the first mention of this special metal. The assessment of silver was the same for each man. To us, the cost of redemption is the same regardless of background or station in life. We all must be redeemed by the blood of our Lord Jesus (see 1 Pet. 1:18–19).

The pins and cords securing the pillar show us Christ, tested in all points (see Heb. 4:15), yet standing firm to become our Savior. The pins without the cords would do nothing to hold the pillars upright. Neither would the cords be effective without a base to secure them. The believer today needs this kind of twofold security if he is to

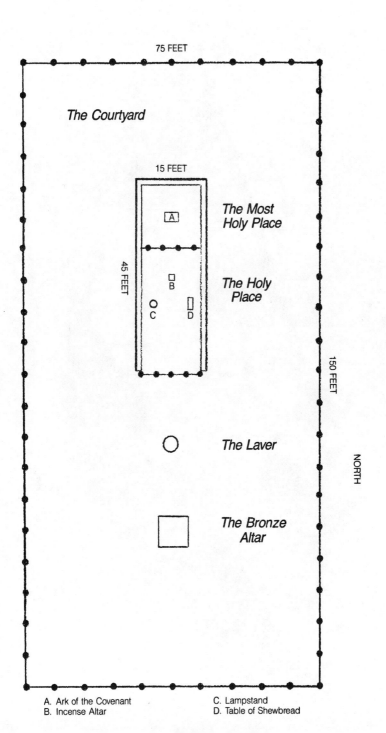

75 FEET

The Courtyard

15 FEET

The Most
Holy Place

A

45 FEET

The Holy
Place

B

C

D

150 FEET

The Laver

NORTH

The Bronze
Altar

A. Ark of the Covenant   C. Lampstand
B. Incense Altar   D. Table of Shewbread

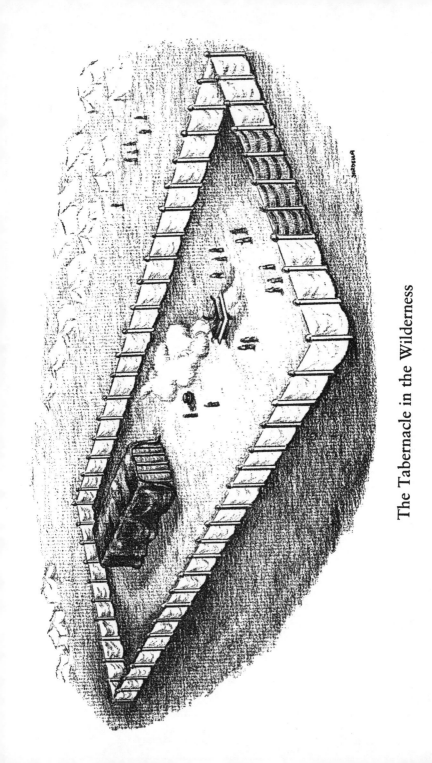

The Tabernacle in the Wilderness

"stand firm" (see Eph. 6:13–19). The two final pieces of our armor are "the sword of the Spirit, which is the word of God", and "all prayer and petition" (Eph. 6:17–18). As the believer spends time daily reading the Word and in prayer, he finds that his fellowship with God is deepened and he is steadied against being "tossed here and there . . . by every wind of doctrine" (Eph. 4:14).

There is another picture before us in the fence. We may also see the pillars as the believers standing under God's judgment for their sins. They are holding up the righteousness of Christ as their only claim, in perfect dress and with the silver crown of redemption alone showing above the linen (see 1 Cor. 1:30).

Regardless of the direction of approach, the Israelites arrived at the gate. It was inescapable. It was the only way into the court and closed the barrier against any frivolous attempts to enter. An embroidered thirty foot long linen piece with the colors of purple, scarlet, and blue on the white linen marked the entry way. Here again we see Jesus in His spotless humanity and His offices as King and sacrificial Lamb of heavenly origin. In this gate Christ is shown as the "door" (see John 10:7), the only way of entry. A sinner cannot come in any way he or she wishes. That person must come in through God's provided way (see John 3:3; 14:6). There was ample access to the Tabernacle through this gate. There were no restrictions as to wealth, prestige, age, or tribe. It was a wide gate—thirty feet, twice as wide as any other entry in the Tabernacle— for whoever would come; yet it was the *only* gate. It was an accessible gate; always open; never barred; with no forbidding doorkeeper. A child could push the curtain aside and enter. The aged found no barrier to his waning strength; likewise the weak, and the unlearned. It was, most of all, the open gate provided by God. Today God calls us to enter His presence through Christ, the Door: "now is the acceptable time . . . the day of salvation" (2 Cor. 6:2). One might stand outside and admire the beautiful needlework of the gate. He might try to duplicate the magnificent pattern or create his own design, but enter he must if he is to enjoy the redemption provided by God. When we are faced with the claims of Christ, we cannot simply speculate on His philosophy or teachings. We must enter the gate to know the joy of full salvation through putting our trust in Christ alone.

The fence, which pictures Christ, stood between Israel and God. By providing an entrance way, Christ has become a mediator, one who takes an official and accepted position between two parties. A mediator is under bonds to offer something that will satisfy each of the parties. By satisfying the claims of each party, he is able to reconcile them, harmonize their differences, and make them friends. Our Lord Jesus is just such a mediator—,"one mediator also between God and men" (1 Tim. 2:5). "He is also the mediator of a better covenant" (Heb. 8:6). We now come "to Jesus, the mediator of a new covenant, and to the sprinkled blood" (Heb. 12:24).

The Tabernacle was not like a modern revival tent, where people sit down inside. The people stood outside in the court. That outer court was no architectural novelty to David. In Psalm 65:4 the psalmist wrote, "How blessed is the one whom Thou dost choose, and bring men to Thee, to dwell in Thy courts. We will be satisfied with the goodness of Thy house, Thy holy temple." In Psalm 84:2, he cries out, "My soul longed and even yearned for the courts of the Lord." He states, "a day in Thy courts is better than a thousand outside" (Ps. 84:10). And in Psalm 92:12–13, he points to true health by saying, "The righteous man . . . will flourish in the courts of our God."

The fence, with its significance in representing the holiness of God, was four hundred and twenty feet in length, the same length as the inner curtains of the Tabernacle proper. We shall learn much more about those curtains later. The striking similarity for now is that the inner curtains had embroidered on them the cherubim, the guardians of God's holiness. We see from these two items, the fence and the curtains, that God's standards of practical holiness are always the same.

One further word about the fence: the world was shut out, and the Israelite had no reason to enter the court except to bring his sacrifice as required by God. He was making a personal decision to enter. So do we, when we accept God's invitation to receive Jesus as Savior and Redeemer. We take a definite step when we cross the barrier and take God at His word. The world was not permitted inside the enclosure. We, too, are called to a definite separation from the world in our walk with God.

CHAPTER THREE

THE BRONZE ALTAR

EXODUS 27:1–8; 38:1–7

As we begin the study of the bronze altar, we shall be occupied with the sacrifices that were offered thereon. We should never forget that the altar alone did not bring redemption. It was the *sacrifice*, taking the sinner's place and being offered up as a substitute, that satisfied the demands of a holy God.

It is common knowledge that other Near Eastern religions made use of sacrifices to their gods. However, they polluted the ceremony by interjecting child sacrifices, sexual rites, and the treatment of the sacrifice as food for their gods and goddesses.

The Bible records that from earliest times people were aware of a need to offer sacrifices to God. "Abel . . . brought of the firstlings of his flock and of their fat portions. And the Lord had regard for Abel and for his offering" (Gen. 4:4). Noah "built an altar to the Lord . . . and offered burnt offerings on the altar" (Gen. 8:20). Abraham built an altar and presented a sacrifice in response to God's promise of the land (see Gen. 12:7–8). Another time he had the sacrifice of a substitute dramatized for him when, in obedience to God, he was prepared to offer up Isaac, his son. God stopped his hand and pointed out a ram "caught in the thicket by his horns; and Abraham went and took the ram, and offered him up for a burnt offering in the place of his son" (Gen. 22:13). Jacob, at the instruction of God, built an altar at Bethel (see Gen. 35:1,7). We observe from Ezekiel 20:7–8 and 23:8,19,27 that Israel as a whole turned from Jehovah to the worship of the Egyptian gods. However, there was undoubtedly a remnant that remained faithful and offered sacrifices to Jehovah as their fathers had before them. In Moses's contest with Pharaoh, he was instructed by Jehovah to make the point that God wanted His people to go "three days' journey into the wilderness, that we may sacrifice to the Lord our God" (Ex. 3:18; 5:3; 8:27). Moses, at the time of the construction of the Tabernacle, codified the commandments of God concerning sacrifice, the altar, and the service of the priests.

About thirty feet inside the gate stood the bronze altar, the first object to meet the eye. It was a square piece, seven and a half feet on each side and four and a half feet high. Made of acacia wood, it was covered inside and out with bronze plates, much in the manner of modern fire doors. It is important to note that bronze, with a melting point of 1,985°F, was used in the construction of the altar and not brass as earlier translations of the Old Testament have indicated. Brass is an alloy of copper and zinc and is of relatively modern use. On the other hand, bronze is an alloy of copper and tin and has been found in many ancient civilizations. The laminated construction of the altar, bronze over wood, gave it the great heat resistance that was called for by its use. The weight and size of the altar made necessary a substantial wooden frame of at least a two-inch thickness. The fire was at its hottest when the sacrificial animal's body was placed on the altar.

Around the midpoint of the outside of the altar was a

shelf or walkway on which the priests moved as they placed the sacrifices on the altar. At the four corners of the top were horns protruding from the bronze plates. These were used as tie points, by which to "bind the festival sacrifice with cords to the horns of the altar" (Ps. 118:27). The horns were also points of refuge for one whose life might be in danger (1 Kin. 2:28). In the consecration of Aaron and his sons to the priesthood, Moses was instructed to "take some of the blood of the bull and put it on the horns of the altar with your finger" (Ex. 29:12). Thus, it is to be noted that the horns were not merely ornamental, but of significance in the life and worship of Israel.

Inside the altar, about twenty-seven inches down from the top was a grate, again of bronze. The grate protruded through the acacia and bronze shell at the corners and became the four points at which the carrying rings were attached. The sacrifice was placed on the grate with the fire below so that the sacrifice was really *in* the altar and not *on* it.

The altar was placed astride a trench, running east to west, in which the firewood was kindled. The air, entering at ground level, ensured a strong draft and a hot fire for the altar. In addition, access to the altar along its four-and-a-half-foot side was secured by a ramp built from the desert sand, enabling the priest to walk up the walkway and reach into the altar as needed.

When the Israelite wished to present a sacrifice, he took the halter of the animal in his hand and started toward the place where the cloud could be seen. For one whose tent was on the outskirts of the camp, it was quite a journey. As he picked his way through the throng, there was ample time to reflect on the incident—sin or trespass—which had set him on his way. Finally, he cleared the last of the tents

The Bronze Altar

and began the passage across the great assembly area to the gate of the outer court. At the gate, he drew aside the beautifully woven cloth and stepped inside. A few words with the priest assured him that he had brought an acceptable sacrifice. He could now proceed with the requirements set down in the Law. He placed his hand on the head of the animal and named the sin or trespass that he had committed. He took the knife in his hand and cut the throat of the bullock, ram, or goat and saw the blood flow as a life was given up in his place. The body of the animal was then placed on the altar and consumed by the fire. With a truly penitent heart, he would know that the penalty required for his sin had been paid. An innocent substitute had taken his place and paid his penalty—a life for a life.

As we look at the altar, we can clearly see the place of judgment symbolized in the bronze. God showed His divine approval of the first public sacrifices by sending fire to consume the burnt offering and fat on the altar (see Lev. 9:22–24). He further ordered that this fire was not to go out (see Lev. 6:8–9). The altar is a type of the cross where "God's wrath fell upon Christ bearing our sins. Man's unbelief has sought in every way to avoid or mitigate this awful truth. But if Divine wrath fell not on Christ, it must fall on us."[1] It was either the sinner or an innocent substitute who must pay for the sin.

The great fire resistability of the altar reminds us that Christ was strengthened by God to withstand the judgment for sin. The grate, with its subjection to intense heat depicts Christ as enduring the presence of God to judge in holiness, a burning without destruction. These were the unseen sufferings of Christ (see Ps. 22:14; 40:12; 69:20; 102:3,4,9,10).

The cross, like the altar, was and is important. God has

provided the way to life through His Son. Men may turn away from it, but in doing so they only delay the decision about accepting Christ until it may be too late. The cross, like the altar, was and is accessible. God invites you now to accept His Son as your Savior, and even today, nineteen hundred years after Calvary, He reminds us that He would have us "Call upon Him while He is near" (Is. 55:6). God's love in sending Christ to die and Christ's availability do not assure the world's salvation. They are only effective to those who avail themselves of God's offer (see John 6:37).

There is one last (but not least) item to consider—the ashes. When the sacrifice was complete and the fire had consumed the body of the animal, there remained the disposal of the ashes. These were carefully removed into a fire pail and carried to a clean place outside the camp. The ashes were the last trace of the sacrifice and were the unmistakable proof that the sacrifice had been completely made. In like manner, our Lord Jesus, when He had paid the debt for sin, was tenderly taken from the cross and laid in a tomb (a clean place). He was raised the third day as proof that the sacrifice had been accepted.

The four horns point to the four corners of the earth and emphasize that the good news of the Gospel is for all mankind—north, south, east, and west (see Mark 16:15). They also remind us of the cross as a place of refuge from sin and Satan.

When Israel went on the march, the altar was covered with a scarlet cloth and two staves were inserted—one through each pair of rings on either side. The scarlet cloth reminds us of Christ's blood shed for us. The two staves carrying the altar typify to us Christ as both our Savior and Reconciler.

As we remember the journey of the Israelite from his

tent to the Tabernacle, we note that he made a personal decision to make a personal trip to bring a personal substitute for his personal sin. In like manner our decision to accept Christ is a vitally personal one. God is satisfied when we personally accept His Word that Christ is our innocent substitute, dying in our place for our sin. No longer does God look upon us in judgment. Have you made this personal decision?

/

CHAPTER FOUR

THE BRONZE LAVER

EXODUS 30:18–21; 38:8

Between the bronze altar and the Tabernacle building stood an extraordinary structure—a laver made entirely of bronze. There are no dimensions given, no detailed description; no shape is specified. Strangely enough, no cover is described for covering the laver when traveling, and no one family is designated for the care of the laver. For such an important piece in the worship of Israel, there are truly many loose ends. Lest we despair, we can draw some conclusions from the information we have.

In Exodus 30:18 we read of "a laver" and "its base", leading us to believe that there were upper and lower sections. The lower section or base may have been a simple pedestal, but the fact that "Aaron and his sons shall wash their hands and their feet from it" (Ex. 30:19), causes us to believe that the lower part was a container of some sort with a possible plumbing connection with the upper or larger vessel. The size of these two compartments is unknown; however, we can arrive at some idea of their capacity by comparing them with their successor piece in the Temple. There we find that most pieces were larger than in the Tabernacle. We read in 1 Kings 7:23 that the

41

The Bronze Laver

new laver or sea (as it was called) was forty-five feet in circumference and seven and one-half feet high. It rested on the backs of twelve bronze oxen making its total height some ten to twelve feet; it contained 19,600 gallons of water. Just the size alone would prevent washing from the large container. We can conclude, therefore, that there was a lower vessel which was easily accessible. Also, it would appear logical that the laver for the Tabernacle had upper and lower compartments and that it would be about five to six feet in total height.

An interesting point is the source of the material for the laver. In Exodus 38:8 we learn that "he [Bezalel] made the laver of bronze with its base of bronze, from the mirrors of the serving women who served at the doorway of the tent of meeting." Here indeed was an offering of love. The mirrors of those days were sheets of burnished metal and represented many hours of rubbing and polishing. They were costly, and for the women who served to give them up as a freewill offering was indeed a gift of love. An object of vanity and pride became an important part of their worship.

When the priests ministered, they were instructed to wash their hands and their feet from the laver; when they went from the altar to the tent of meeting, they were to wash; when they approached the altar to present the sacrifice, they were to wash. This was not an option. The priests were to wash their hands and their feet "that they may not die; and it shall be a perpetual statute for them, for Aaron and his descendants throughout their generations" (Ex. 30:21).

Lest this laver be regarded as "the village wash stand", we are reminded very clearly that Aaron and his sons were to wash *from* the laver, and not *in* it. Exodus 30:19, in the King James Version, reads they "shall wash their hands and their feet thereat"—again, *at*, not *in*. The command to wash was a constant reminder to the priest that he had become defiled in the act of ministering. He was not to forget that he walked and ministered in the presence of a most holy God.

As we contemplate the laver, the mirrors from which it was made remind us that by looking on them we see our life as God sees it. The whole construction and use of the laver are illustrations of the Word of God working in our lives. There are many symbols for divine revelation in the Word—water (see Eph. 5:26), milk (see 1 Pet. 2:2), a hammer and fire (see Jer. 23:29), and a two-edged sword (see Heb. 4:12). The combination of the mirrors and water is most apt in this point. We look into the Word and see our need of cleansing; then we apply the water to our need and find ourselves refreshed and cleansed—made fit to approach our heavenly Father in prayer and worship.

Of great significance in the use of the laver was the source of the water. Israel had left Egypt behind geographically, but they still lusted after Egypt's creature comforts. So soon had they forgotten the taskmaster's whip. As they reached Rephidim, we are told, "there was no water for the people to drink" (Ex. 17:1). In their rage and frustration they turned on Moses, accusing him of bringing the people out of Egypt to kill them with thirst. Moses cried to God, "A little more and they will stone me" (Ex. 17:4). God's reply was to calm his servant and instruct him to take his rod in his hand, and with the elders of Israel, to stand on the rock at Horeb. He was not to stand alone. "I will stand before you there on the rock," (Ex. 17:6) said Jehovah. Moses struck the rock in the sight of Israel and water came out—gushed out—in a stream for the people to drink—all 2,000,000 of them. The New Testament commentary on this incident is found in 1 Cor. 10:4, where (speaking of Israel) Paul says, by the Holy Spirit, "They were drinking from a spiritual rock which followed them; and the rock was Christ." Water was at a premium in the desert, but here was the God of Abraham supplying their need through the second person of the Godhead, even our Lord Jesus. The people's thirst was slaked, and the priests had the water applied to their defilement. It was God Himself who was the water of cleansing so that the priest could be prepared for worship and return to the people to minister at the altar.

The location of the laver was significant. It was placed between the altar and the Tent of Meeting. Thus, it could not be bypassed by the priest; whether going into the Tabernacle to worship or returning to minister at the altar, he was commanded to stop and wash.

Today, the child of God must not neglect the Word if he is to have rich fellowship with God and be fruitful in sharing the good news of the gospel. Just rubbing shoulders with those around us makes it necessary for cleansing. It is easy to absorb unwittingly the world's values and philosophy. Before telling others about our Savior, let us turn daily to the Word that our witness may be positive and effective.

It is important at this moment that we pause to consider a fact not known to all believers. Among the many things that happen to a person immediately upon his receiving Christ as his personal Savior is the fact that each and every believer becomes a priest unto God (see 1 Pet. 2:9–10). John, in the Revelation, confirms this priesthood by citing what Christ has done in making "us to be a kingdom, priests to His God and Father" (Rev. 1:6). The twenty-four elders repeat, "And Thou hast made them to be a kingdom and priests to our God" (Rev. 5:10).

It is in the office of believer-priest that we can tell the

good news of the gospel. In this way we minister at the altar by pointing to the cross where the Son of God paid the full penalty for sin. As the believer-priest moves into a time of worship, he needs the cleansing of the Word that his worship might be with a full heart. We shall see more of this privilege of priesthood as we move inside the building.

In applying the Word of God to our lives, we find that the hindrance to ministry is removed. In like manner, the application of the Word to our lives removes any hindrance to worship. As we go to prayer (and we go on scriptural ground), we find our times of petition and intercession to be much deeper and fuller.

The Word in our lives functions in many blessed ways:[1]

1. It provides faith (see Rom. 10:17). This presumes that we are heeding the Word (see Heb. 2:1). We don't originate faith; God gives it by hearing.
2. It provides a defense (see Eph. 6:17). It is the sword of the Spirit, the Word of God that enables us to stand (see Eph. 6:13). Satan would interfere with our worship but the sword is a sure defense.
3. It provides growth. We are exhorted to "grow in the grace and knowledge of our Lord" (2 Pet. 3:18). Paul calls us "to grow up in all aspects into Him" (Eph. 4:15).
4. It provides discernment. The Word is "able to judge the thoughts and intentions of the heart" (Heb. 4:12).
5. It provides power. We have access to God's creative power. "It shall be done for you" (John 15:7). This verse means for the believer "If it isn't around, I'll make it for you."
6. It provides instruction. The Scripture is "profitable for teaching" (2 Tim. 3:16).

At this point we should draw some comparisons (beyond the obvious physical differences) between the laver and the altar.[2]

The Laver	The Altar
For believer-priests only	For everyone
For water	For fire
Cleansing agent—water	Cleansing agent—blood
Points to the Word of God	Points to the cross—sacrifice
Present sins dealt with	Past sins dealt with
Ministry done by the priest	Ministry done for the priest
Provided because of ministry	Priesthood ministry made possible

In Exodus 30:21 we have the final instructions regarding the use of the laver. The last clause reads, "and it shall be a perpetual statute for them, for Aaron and his descendants throughout their generations." With this injunction ringing in our ears, we search in vain for any other reference to the laver. When Solomon built the Temple, he substituted "a sea of cast metal" (1 Kin. 7:23); but the laver from the Tabernacle is not mentioned. This is a sad fact to recount. In the period of time from Sinai to Solomon's temple, the laver was in disuse and the virus of Israel's decline was on the increase. The Christian who neglects the reading of his Bible (his time at the laver) stands in the same peril of spiritual decline as did Israel. Samuel sets us an example of the believer who is careful about his spiritual health. We read that, ". . . Samuel grew, and the Lord was with him, and did let none of his words fall to the ground" (1 Sam. 3:19 KJV). Oh, that God would give us a similar attitude toward the things of God!

CHAPTER FIVE

THE CURTAINS AND COVERINGS

EXODUS 26:1–14; 36:8–19

"The ark of God dwells within tent curtains" (2 Sam. 7:2). This was David's complaint to Nathan as he sought some way to improve the surroundings of the worship of Jehovah and make it comparable to his own "house of cedar".

In the itinerant life of Israel, curtains were a very practical part of the Tabernacle. It is through these four draperies of textile, hair, and skin, one above the other, that God would teach us some very practical lessons.

The inner curtain was woven of linen of the byssus type referred to earlier. There were actually ten curtains, each forty-two feet by six feet. The six feet seems to have been the loom width that they had to use. The ten curtains were divided into two groups of five each, and the individual curtains of each five were joined at their selvedges making two large curtains measuring forty-two feet by thirty feet. On one edge of each of the large curtains there were fifty loops of blue. The goldsmiths were to fashion fifty clasps which would be used to join the two large curtains along their thirty-foot sides when in place. This joining would take place over the pillars of the veil, about which we shall learn more later.

The interior of the Tabernacle measured forty-five feet in length, by fifteen feet in width, by fifteen feet in height. This meant that the curtains were loosely draped in both rooms and that an additional ten to twelve feet hung down over the back. The forty-two foot width would come to within a very few feet from the ground on either side. This made the Tabernacle one perfect whole.

The design of the curtain was dictated to Bezalel or Oholiab (whichever one was in charge of this part of the project): "You shall make the tabernacle with ten curtains of fine twisted linen and blue and purple and scarlet material; you shall make them with cherubim, the work of a skillful workman" (Ex. 26:1). This last phrase implies the work of a thinking man, one who is inventive and who works with divine guidance.

"With cherubim?" Bezalel might ask. "Where do I get a pattern for this?" Then he would remember Moses's words to him; God had said "I have called by name Bezalel. . . . I have filled him with the Spirit of God in wisdom, in understanding, in knowledge . . . to make artistic designs" (Ex. 31:1–4). So he would go to work.

In blue, scarlet, and purple they embroidered the form of cherubim throughout the curtain. These angelic beings were of the highest order, each with the faces of a man, a lion, an ox, and an eagle (see Ezek. 1:6,10) and were charged with guarding the holiness of God (see Gen. 3:24). The faces symbolized a variety of characteristics: in the man was seen intellect, mind, knowledge, and personal will; in the lion, kingly dignity, power, and glory; in the ox, strength for service; in the eagle, the ability to soar to great heights and power for supreme perception. It was quite fitting that these creatures be seen many times in the ceiling hanging of the rooms where acknowledgement of the holiness of God was paramount.

The colors used in the basic material and the embroidery picture our Lord Jesus. The white linen stands for His spotless humanity. At His birth He was called "the holy offspring" (Luke 1:35). He had an encounter with a Pharisee and a harlot and remained unspotted (see John 8:3–4). At His crucifixion, Pilate found "no guilt in this man" (Luke 23:14). One of the criminals crucified with Him said, "This man hath done nothing wrong" (Luke 23:41). The final testimony came from the centurion: "Certainly this man was innocent" (Luke 23:47).

Jesus's heavenly source, symbolized in the blue color, is most clearly seen in John's gospel. In John 1:14, we read that "the Word became flesh, and dwelt among us." In 3:13 He declares Himself to be the one "who descended from heaven." He identifies Himself in 6:58 as "the bread which came down out of heaven". In 13:3 we also read, "He had come forth from God, and was going back to God".

As for the kingly purple, Jesus's life on earth began with the wise men asking, "Where is He who has been born King of the Jews?" (Matt. 2:2). In Matthew, the constitution of the King is declared, and the works of the King are displayed. In chapter 21, He makes His triumphal entry; and in chapter 22, He tells the parable of the king's wedding feast being open to all. In chapters 24 and 25, we see the King speaking of His glory; and in chapter 27, we view the King crucified. But the King arose, and He commissioned His disciples and gave them all authority as it had been given Him (see Matt. 28:18).

The scarlet, for the perfect servant, is appropriate for the Gospel of Mark. The identifying word in Mark is "immediately"—the servant responding promptly and without question. Also, Paul pointed out Christ's role as a servant in Phil. 2:7–8: "[He] emptied Himself, taking the form of a bond-servant, and being made in the likeness of men. And being found in appearance as a man, He humbled Himself by becoming obedient to the point of death, even death on a cross." What a complete picture of a servant this brings to us! Before leading Him out for crucifixion in preparing Him for His ultimate duty as the Servant, "they stripped Him, and put a scarlet robe on Him" (Matt. 27:28).

Thus we can see in these four colors, the themes of the four Gospels:

1. White—Luke: Christ, the Son of Man
2. Blue—John: Christ, the Son of God
3. Purple—Matthew: Christ, the King
4. Scarlet—Mark: Christ, the obedient Servant,
   faithful unto death

The curtains had loops of blue added to their edges so that they could be assembled without marring the pattern of the cherubim. The union of the curtains was completed by the use of golden clasps. Since these curtains in their design and colors point to our Lord Jesus, we look upon the loops of heavenly blue and upon the clasps as the uniting of our Lord Jesus with needy mankind.

As we consider the golden clasps we find a remarkable use of the word translated "clasp." It comes from a verb meaning "to stoop, to bend." These clasps show us our Lord Jesus in the gold of His deity, stooping to man in order to unite him with a holy God. This is grace in action. God stooped to become man (see John 1:14) that He might bear our sins and raise us to become sons of God.

We shall see more of the cherubim as we study the

furniture of the Holy Place. The figures in the curtains looked down on the ministering priest to be the constant reminder of God's holiness.

The next covering was one for durability rather than beauty. "You shall make curtains of goats' hair for a tent over the tabernacle; you shall make eleven curtains in all" (Ex. 26:7). The cloth was woven from the hair of the black eastern goat. Not only could the hair be taken directly from the goat, but there existed a children's industry of gleaning goats' hair from the bushes among which the animals wandered in search of food. Part of the goat herder's duty, which still exists today, was to see that this deposit of hair did not go to waste. The hair was spun into thread by the women and then made into a closely woven cloth.

Like the linen, the cloth was woven on the six-foot wide loom in strips that were forty-five feet in length. Those strips were joined along their sides into larger curtains of five and six strips. The two curtains also had fifty loops at the point where they would join, and fifty clasps of bronze to complete the joining. They were draped over the inner curtain and the body of the building, with the extra length and width being allowed to go over the back and sides. The sixth strip of the larger curtain was to be doubled back over the front of the Tabernacle. This was definitely designed as a protective covering. Since this, or a similar material, was used in making a tent dwelling (Song 1:5), it could be counted upon to keep out the weather.

The goat was important as a sacrificial animal. When an Israelite came with a guilt offering for a sin he had committed, he was instructed to "bring . . . a female from the flock, a lamb or a goat as a sin offering" (Lev. 5:6). (We have seen how personally the Israelite became involved in the sin offering). Also, at the consecration of the priests, a goat was among the specified animals (see Lev. 9:3,5). On the Day of Atonement, two goats were "for a sin offering" (Lev. 16:5). Lots were cast and one goat became a sin offering, while the other goat became the scapegoat, and was sent into the wilderness (see Lev. 16:9,10). Finally, at the dedication of the altar, a goat was specified as part of the offering each of the leaders of Israel was commanded to bring (see Num. 7:16).

In the Hebrew tongue, one of the words for sin is also the word for sin offering. In the New Testament, the sin offering is the Lamb of God being made "sin on our behalf, that we might become the righteousness of God in Him" (2 Cor. 5:21).

We noted that the clasps used on the goats' hair curtain were of bronze, while those of the inner curtain were of gold. Throughout the Tabernacle, gold and bronze were not used together. In the outer court where judgment was the theme, bronze was the predominant metal; but within the Tabernacle, gold was used exclusively. We shall learn some special things about gold as we move into the Tabernacle, but it is entirely consistent that gold (deity) should be used in connection with the inner curtains and bronze for the goats' hair curtains (one layer removed from the interior and unseen) which spoke of judgment.

The third covering is described and specified in just fourteen English words—"And you shall make a covering for the tent of rams' skins dyed red" (Ex. 26:14). There are no directions as to size other than "a covering" nor are there directions as to joining the many skins required to complete the covering, but prepare "the covering" they did. They likely used leather thongs as a thread, an ancient practice.

The most poignant illustration of the ram is the account of Abraham's trusting journey with Isaac to the mountain in the land of Moriah. Isaac's question about the seeming lack in preparation for the sacrifice received the astounding answer from his father, "God will provide for Himself the lamb for the burnt offering, my son" (Gen. 22:8). This seemed to end the conversation. At the crucial moment God had caused a ram to become entangled in a thicket. God provided a sacrifice similar to the later requirement of a "lamb for the burnt offering." The use of the skin of this animal was God's signature on the Tabernacle indicating His full provision for atonement for sin.

The ram was used in the burnt offering (Lev. 9:2), in the peace offering (Lev. 9:18), and in the guilt offering (Lev. 5:16). In the consecration of the priests, the ram was a central part of the ceremony for setting apart their ears, hands, and feet to the service of God.

Our Lord Jesus was as completely devoted as the symbol of the ram would indicate. He came into the world with a body prepared to do His Father's will (see Heb. 10:5–7). He laid down His life for us. It was His initiative. "No one has taken it away from Me, but I lay it down on My own initiative. I have authority to lay it down, and I have authority to take it up again. This commandment I received from My Father" (John 10:18). When His hour came He did not turn aside: "For this purpose I came to this hour" (John 12:27). We read the comforting words of John 14 in times of grief, but we can easily miss the two words that make the comfort possible—"I go" (v. 28). I GO! Our Savior said this, knowing well the road that lay ahead; the mockery, the torment, the spitting, and finally the separation from God as He became sin for us (see 2 Cor. 5:21).

The outermost covering was of porpoises' skins (see Ex. 26:14). This mammal was in plentiful supply in the Red Sea and the Nile delta. It was widely used for sandals (see

Ezek. 16:10) and formed an important part of the protective coverings of the furniture of the Tabernacle when Israel was on the move (see Num. 4:6,8,10–12). It was dull of color and served as a perfect protection against all kinds of adverse weather conditions. It gave no indication of the beauty inside the structure. This beauty was reserved for those who would enter; having come in God's way.

In Isaiah we have this description of our Lord Jesus: "His appearance was marred more than any man, and His form more than the sons of men" (Is. 52:14). And again, "He has no stately form or majesty that we should look upon Him, nor appearance that we should be attracted to Him" (Is. 53:2). Mankind looks upon the Son of God as just a teacher, an example, a revolutionary, a dreamer—these are their labels. To those who know Him and have received Him by faith, however, He is the "rose of Sharon, the lily of the valleys" (Song 2:1); "He is altogether lovely" (Song 5:16 KJV).

As people look at the life of believers, they should see Christ's beauty and His loveliness. As Paul says in his second letter to the Corinthians, we are letters of Christ, "Written not with ink, but with the Spirit of the living God . . . on tablets of human hearts" (2 Cor. 3:3). What kind of a story do they receive? Colorless? Unexciting? Meaningless? Since it "is Christ in you, the hope of glory" (Col. 1:27), those around us will see what is written in our lives. Let us turn again to be filled with Christ through the Holy Spirit and so show others the beauty they can see no other way.

> Let the beauty of Jesus be seen in me,
>   All His wonderful passion and purity;
> O Thou Spirit divine,
>   All my nature refine,
> 'Till the beauty of Jesus be seen in me!

CHAPTER SIX

THE DOOR

EXODUS 26:36–37

The priest has just completed the washing of his hands and feet at the laver. He now turns toward the main structure which stands before him. It is draped on three sides with the drab coverings of porpoises' skins, but in beautiful contrast, the "screen for the doorway of the tent" (Ex. 26:36) is immediately in the line of vision. It, too, is made with the four colors of blue, purple, scarlet, and fine twisted linen (white). It is interesting to notice that wherever these colors are mentioned in connection with the Tabernacle and the garments of the priests, the colors, with one exception, are always listed in this order.

We have considered the significance of these colors in previous chapters. One other matter of aesthetics or harmony attracts our attention. The use of blue (sky blue) and scarlet together in a pattern can produce a jarring effect on the eyes. In the hangings of the Tabernacle and the garments of the high priest, the addition of purple, which is formed by the combining of blue and scarlet, provides a bridge between the other two colors resulting in a pleasing effect to the eye. "God is not a God of confusion" (1 Cor.

14:33) and attention to the detail of a pleasing color effect is further evidence of His order.

The doorway was woven with strands of the four colors. Nothing is said about the pattern except to indicate that it was variegated. Notably, there were no cherubim, those guardians of God's holiness whose presence would have made the doorway into a barrier.

The doorway was narrower than the gate of the court; but still it was fifteen feet wide and fifteen feet high and stood as an invitation to the priest to enter for worship.

In considering the gate, we saw the Lord Jesus as "the way" (see John 14:6). The doorway may signify our Lord as "the truth." Dr. I. M. Haldeman has made the following comments:

> The hanging was a door, but it was also a revelation, a revelation of the truth concerning the Tabernacle.
>
> When the priest passed under the hanging he was face to face with the golden symbols within. In these symbols he saw the truth of God's way in grace, in redemption and glory. Outside of that hanging he could not know the truth of the Tabernacle, the truth it alone could reveal.
>
> Our Lord Jesus Christ is the antitype of all that. He is the revelation of God. He is the revelation of God as the Father. He is the revelation of God as the God of infinite love.
>
> He reveals Him as the God of measureless grace. He reveals Him as a God who is able to save unto the uttermost all who come unto Him by faith in His crucified, self-immolated and risen Son. He reveals Him as the God of glory, the God who will give grace and glory and no good thing will He withhold from them who put their trust in Him.
>
> He is the full and complete disclosure of God.
>
> He is the truth about God.

He is the truth of God.
He is the God of truth.
He is God manifest in the flesh.
Since He is God in the flesh and the truth of God, He is entitled to say, "I am the truth" and fittingly does the hanging which revealed the truth of the Tabernacle symbolize Him as the truth.[1]

The curtained doorway was suspended from five pillars equally spaced across the fifteen-foot width. The pillars were of shittim wood, covered with gold, and resting on sockets of bronze. The capitals of the columns and the connecting bars were of silver, while the hooks to hold the curtain were of gold. Those pillars show us our Lord Jesus as the Redeemer God, bearing judgment in our place.

That there were five columns is no accident. Neither is it an accident that there were five writers of the Epistles—James, John, Jude, Paul, and Peter. The Epistles constitute our book of worship; and these five writers, by the Holy Spirit, hold up our Lord Jesus as the One to whom all worship is due. At least three of these men are described as "pillars" (see Gal. 2:9). Their writing shows us "how one ought to conduct himself in the household of God, which is the church of the living God" (1 Tim. 3:15). Once we have been to the altar and placed our trust in Christ as Savior and gone on to the laver for daily washing in the Word of God, our feet should naturally turn to worship our wonderful Lord. "The love of Christ controls us" (2 Cor. 5:14), and we find ourselves longing for a closer walk with Him.

A few words on the nature of our worship are appropriate here. Worship is the acknowledgement of God's worth. The word "worship" is derived from an earlier Anglo-Saxon word, "worth ship." The difficult letters were

The Doorway to the Holy Place

dropped over the years to give us our current word "worship." Worship does not consist solely in stated meetings in a finely appointed church building nor in robed choirs and inspirational music. Worship is the out-flow of the individual's heart in a myriad of different ways and in the most unpredictable circumstances. The whole of our life as believers should be a continuing act of worship.

As we read the Word (and it should be done daily), we are acknowledging that His word is valuable and has something to say to us that we should heed. As we go through the day, the perfume of the moments spent in reading and meditation will rise to beautify many a dull moment. The prayer time, when we speak to God, is not limited to set periods—although a regular habit of prayer is important. At any moment, the Holy Spirit can and does bring to our mind some promise that we have claimed or should claim, or some person going through a time of struggle who needs our prayer. Our hearts will answer in a moment of worship, acknowledging God's goodness in reminding us of this. Our time of worship in this case can be between the touch of one typewriter key and the next, or between one sentence and another in the midst of a telephone conversation. The meeting with others, "who have received a faith of the same kind as ours" (2 Pet. 1:1), can be the work of God's hand. A few words together reveals the bond in the gospel, and we may go on our way thanking God for bringing them across our path.

In Hebrews, we are instructed, "Through Him then, let us continually offer up a sacrifice of praise to God, that is, the fruit of lips that give thanks to His name" (Heb. 13:15). How about the fruit of our lips? Does it qualify as "a sacrifice of praise"? Without being sanctimonious about it, we must admit that our daily speech betrays the degree to which we acknowledge God's rule in our lives. A sacrifice of praise? This praise is not the pat on the head we might give to a child for a lesson well done; this praise is worship. We can and should worship with the words that pass our lips.

Peter, in his first epistle (1 Pet. 4:11) says, "Whoever speaks, . . . whoever serves, let him do so as by the strength which God supplies; so that in all things God may be glorified through Jesus Christ." Has God given you a ministry large or small? He would have you discharge it in His strength, not your erudition. When we do it with the strength that God gives, He is glorified. When we acknowledge that God has supplied the strength and the wisdom for the task, the results are entirely in His hands.

Some years ago I saw over the kitchen sink of a dear child of God, a motto which read, "Divine services performed here three times daily." This is very practical worship. Should not this attitude also be yours while sitting at a desk, operating a machine, driving a truck or taxi cab, or whatever your daily task might be?

In Malachi 3:16 we read, "Then those who feared the Lord spoke to one another, and the Lord gave attention and heard it, and a book of remembrance was written before Him for those who fear the Lord and who esteem His name." In the King James Version, the word "esteem" is translated "thought on"—a book of remembrance for those who "thought on" His name. Here is a time of worship that requires no formal preparation or elaborate ritual and is placed in God's book of remembrance. He also gives attention and hears it.

The real test of worship comes when we are exhorted to be "always giving thanks for all things in the name of our Lord Jesus Christ, to God, even the Father" (Eph. 5:20).

All things? Yes, all things—the good with the bad, the pleasant with the unpleasant, the defeats with the victories.

A young pastor and his wife were expecting their first child. There was the happy anticipation: the playful debate over "boy or girl", the preparation of the nursery, and, of course, much prayer. The happy day came, and the husband drove his wife to the hospital for the climactic hours. Soon they would have the answer. Then the blow fell. The child was mongoloid! "But God—?" But God sent a wiser, older man of God to the young pastor's home on that very day. He went to his younger friend and, putting his arm around his shoulder, said, "Read this with me—'always giving thanks for all things in the name of our Lord Jesus' [Eph. 5:20]. If you can do this now, your ministry will be blessed beyond your dreams." The two men fell to their knees and poured out their hearts to God who does all things well. God blessed the young pastor and his wife with several normal children in addition to the exceptional child they loved and cared for. But best of all, God sent His servant from that trying hour to a life of powerful spiritual ministry across this country. When we can sing the Doxology through our tears, that is true worship.

There is an additional precious thought. When the child of God has put away sin at the altar and washed at the laver, he may, with confidence, enter through the doorway of truth for worship. This is a peculiarly private time which fits each individual believer. We have seen some of the ways of worship, but to each one it is given to worship in the manner that is distinctively his or hers. There is no prescribed ritual. It is a time between the individual believer and God.

The gate to the outer court excluded all who would not come to the altar in God's appointed way. The doorway was not intended as a barrier but rather as an invitation. However, entering into the Holy Place meant that the heart of the worshiper must be deeply moved to desire the real intimacy of a time alone with God. Today, also, should the believer retain some unconfessed sin or some portion of pride despite the confession at the altar, he will find worship a time when the Holy Spirit cries out against carnal pride and sin; a din of conflict will be the portion of that worshiper. "He who comes to God must believe that He is, and that He is a rewarder of those who seek Him" (Heb. 11:6).

> O could I speak the matchless worth,
> O could I sound the glories forth
>   Which in my Saviour shine,
> I'd soar and touch the heavenly strings
> And vie with Gabriel while he sings
>   In notes almost divine.
>
> I'd sing the precious blood He spilt
> My ransom from the dreadful guilt
>   Of sin, and wrath divine;
> I'd sing His glorious righteousness,
> In which all perfect, heavenly dress
>   My soul shall ever shine.
>
> I'd sing the characters He bears,
> And all the forms of love He wears,
>   Exalted on His throne;
> In loftiest songs of sweetest praise,
> I would to everlasting days
>   Make all His glories known.
>
> Well, the delightful day will come
> When my dear Lord will bring me home
>   And I shall see His face;

Then with my Saviour, Brother, Friend,
A blest eternity I'll spend,
  Triumphant in His grace.

                                    Samuel Medley

CHAPTER SEVEN

THE BOARDS AND BARS

EXODUS 26:15–30; 36:20–34

As the priest pushed aside the "curtain for the doorway," he found himself inside the Tabernacle building. Whether this were his first or his fiftieth trip inside the building, he would be overwhelmed by the beauty that met his eyes—the golden furniture, the inner curtain, the majestic veil, and the walls of gold. How could he not fall to his knees in worship?

The walls were fitted together with boards twenty-seven inches wide and fifteen feet long. Each one was made of acacia wood and was covered with gold. There has been considerable debate as to the thickness of the boards. Scripture is silent on these dimensions. Some hold the thickness tapered from eighteen inches at the bottom to three inches at the top. A generally accepted dimension is eighteen inches from top to bottom.

The dimensions of the boards and the use of the word *make* bring us face to face with the fact that the acacia tree is not large enough to produce timbers of the size described. That timbers of these dimensions could be assembled (laminated) is stupendous. When we realize that this was part of "all that I am going to show you" (Ex.

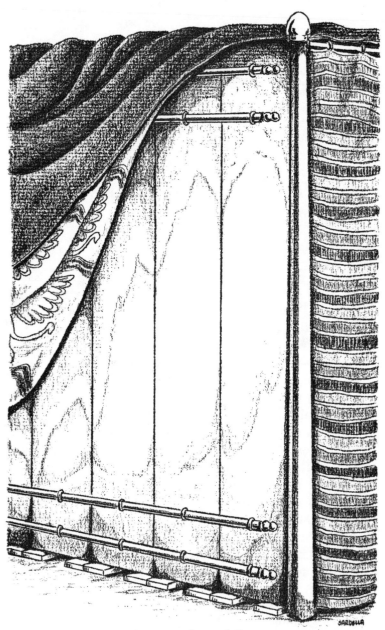

The Boards and Bars

25:9), it is the more remarkable that it should be part of the divine plan and process.

There were 48 boards required for the building—20 for each of the north and south sides, 6, plus 2 special corner boards, for the western end of the structure. These special boards seem to have been made as though one specially made board had been split and beveled at a 45 degree angle along the 15 foot sides and joined in an "L" shape to form a usable timber. As we shall see, the inside dimensions of the Tabernacle were 45 feet in length and 15 feet in width. The six boards assigned to the western end provided a total of 6 x 27 inches or 162 inches. The 9 inch projections from the two corner boards added exactly 18 inches to the length of the western end inside dimensions to provide 180 inches or 15 feet.

What about the sides? The twenty boards indicated totaled 540 inches or 45 feet, but there were an additional 9 inches from the corner board. Fifteen feet from the western wall was the veil with its pillars. Nine inches would be a reasonable allowance for pillars strong enough to support the veil. Now we have 30 feet from the veil to the doorway and 15 feet from the veil to the western wall. He who calls the stars by name took care of a matter of 9 inches in the Tabernacle made according to the pattern shown to Moses on the mountain.

Each of the forty-eight boards had two tenons on its lower end. The word "tenon" also means "hands." This idea has an interesting and blessed meaning as we shall see. Each of the tenons fitted into the mortises of a silver base, which supplied firmness wherever the building was assembled. For the forty-eight boards, there were ninety-six bases that were made from the silver of the redemption money.

To add to the strength of the structure there were five

rods along each of the three sides. The rods were of acacia wood covered with gold. Four of the rods were placed through rings in the outer surfaces of the boards. Between the external rods there was one rod that ran inside the boards the entire forty-five foot length of the side walls and the fifteen foot length of the western wall. Those rods added greatly to the stability of the building.

We now have the complete picture of the building consisting of the large timbers with tenons fixed in bases of silver, buttressed by the rods, internal and external, the specially coupled corner boards, and the additional cross strengthening by the fillets of the pillars at the doorway and the veil. These walls bore the weight of the coverings described in Chapter V and helped sustain the doorway and the veil.

As we look upon the boards there are many things God would have us see. First, the acacia wood came from the desert-grown tree that finds its sustenance through deep roots. Here is the humanity of Christ, the "root out of parched ground" (Is. 53:2). He took upon Himself a human body, prepared for Him in order that He might bring many to glory and perform the will of his Father (see Heb. 10:5). We read that "since then the children share in flesh and blood, He Himself likewise also partook of the same" (Heb. 2:14). This gives us the picture of the eternal Christ experiencing the laying aside of His glory to accomplish the Father's purpose. When Mary was visited by Gabriel, who announced that she was to give birth to a son, she first presumed that it would be a natural conception and birth. But she was told that she had "found favor with God", and would "bear a son and . . . name Him Jesus" (Luke 1:30,31). The marvel of the angel's announcement came with the words, "The Holy Spirit will come upon you, and the power of the Most High will overshadow you; and for that reason the holy offspring shall be called the Son of God" (Luke 1:35). In crossing the bridge of time and space, Christ gave up none of His essential deity nor was His humanity any less distinct.

All during His years of ministry, Jesus showed His humanity. He became hungry and thirsty, and He ate and drank. At Lazarus's tomb He wept. These were human tears. He died and was buried in the same way other human beings were buried.

Even as He walked with human beings, however, He was not contaminated by them. He was "holy, innocent, undefiled, separated from sinners and exalted above the heavens" (Heb. 7:26). He confronted the religious teachers of the day with the challenge, "Which one of you convicts Me of sin?" (John 8:46). The writer to the Hebrews characterized Him as "one who has been tempted in all things as we are, yet without sin" (Heb. 4:15). Two of His disciples, John and Peter, who were with Him over three years, bore witness that "in Him there is no sin" (1 John 3:5), and that He "committed no sin nor was any deceit found in His mouth" (1 Pet. 2:22). Lest these witnesses be considered prejudiced, we listen to a hardened military man whose only interest was in carrying out the sentence of death. His words were, "Certainly this man was innocent" (Luke 23:47), and he praised God. Truly He was man of very man but holy and without sin.

The boards of the Tabernacle walls were overlaid with gold. It completely covered the sides of the boards; yet the metal did not invade the wood, nor did the wood displace the gold. There was no mixing of Christ's deity with his humanity. He maintained from the beginning a claim that "He who has seen me has seen the Father" (John 14:9). Paul refers to Him as "our great God and Savior, Christ Jesus" (Titus 2:13). It is a mystery, but an important one, that the two natures existed, but the one never invaded the other.

The Gospel accounts are filled with demonstrations of the divine power of our Lord. After the village wedding at Cana where Jesus turned water to wine, John made this comment: "This beginning of His signs Jesus did in Cana of Galilee, and manifested His glory, and His disciples believed in Him" (John 2:11). At the end of his Gospel, John wrote, "Many other signs therefore Jesus also performed in the presence of His disciples, which are not written in this book; but these have been written that you may believe that Jesus is the Christ, the Son of God; and that believing you may have life in His name" (John 20:30–31). Truly, the Man Christ Jesus was none other than God our Savior. "Great is the mystery of godliness: He who was revealed in the flesh, was vindicated in the Spirit, beheld by angels, proclaimed among the nations, believed on in the world, taken up in glory" (1 Tim. 3:16).

Dr. Donald Grey Barnhouse was one of God's choice servants. His ability to illumine truth was superb. He told of a legend of an Irish king who disguised himself and went into the banquet hall of one of his barons. He was escorted to a lowly place among the throng who sat at the feast. The brilliance of his conversation and the nobility of his manner soon attracted the attention of someone with sufficient authority to escort him to a higher table. The same thing occurred once more, and soon he was seated among the nobles of the realm. After a display of great wisdom, one of the lords spoke out and said, "In truth, sir, you speak like a king. If you are not a king, you deserve to be." Then the king removed his disguise, was recognized as the king, and took his rightful place among his subjects. Dr. Barnhouse continues,

When our Lord Jesus came from heaven's glory, His subjects were so blinded by their own darkness of heart that
they were not willing to stoop before Him. The King of
Kings and Lord of Lords was there, but they received Him
not, even though He stated over and over again that He
was the eternal God come down to redeem them.[1]

Continuing our examination of the structure of the Tabernacle, we learn that the boards stood upright, each board
with its two tenons in its two bases of silver that kept the
boards from tipping over despite the nature of the ground
on which the Tabernacle was erected, be it desert sand or
stony ground. The two tenons reached deep into their
settings to hold fast the structure.

The silver for the bases, which came from the redemption money of the census, reminds us once more of the
Lord Jesus who as "our great God and Savior, Christ Jesus
. . . gave Himself for us, that He might redeem us from
every lawless deed and purify for Himself a people for His
own possession" (Titus 2:13–14).

The four external bars and rings of gold plus the one
internal bar added the final touch of stability to the building. It was essential that these walls stand firm under their
load of hangings and against the forces of the weather.

Rev. Arthur W. Pink writes,

The relation of the boards to the Tabernacle, to its holy
vessels, and to the ministrations of the priests therein,
supplies the key to their distinctive significance. Without
these boards there had been no Tabernacle to house its
furniture and no place for the priests to serve in. Moreover,
without them the beautiful curtains could not have been
displayed. The golden boards, held together by the golden
bars, resting in their silver sockets, sustained all the weight

of the curtains and coverings. So on the God-man was hung all the weight of the divine government and all the glories of His Father's house. . . .

That which is foreshadowed in the boards is the Person of Christ as that which sustained His work. The massive framework of the golden boards was to the curtains and coverings suspended from them, what the poles are to the tent.[2]

If Christ were not man of very man and God of very God, His saving work would have been in vain.

Another lesson is waiting for us in the boards when they symbolize believers. We grow up in the barrenness of this world; we draw our needs from it; we bend before the forces of the god of this world, and our nature is full of the knots and twists of our natural state. But God wished to do something wonderful. He sent His Son to give His life for us and pluck us out of the arid and fruitless life. He causes us to stand upright having laid a foundation of redemption for each one. Our hands "take hold of the eternal life to which [we] were called" (1 Tim. 6:12). We have the gold (deity) of His new nature within us. As bars to sustain our position He has given us "apostles, . . . prophets, and some as evangelists, and some as pastors and teachers" (Eph. 4:11). Day by day we find support and stability from others whom God has called to come into our life so that "we are to grow up in all aspects into Him, who is the head, even Christ, from whom the whole body, being fitted and held together by that which every joint supplies, according to the proper working of each individual part, causes the growth of the body for the building up of itself in love" (Eph. 4:15–16).

The middle bar, unseen from the outside, pictures for us the unifying work of the Holy Spirit as he "Himself bears witness with our spirit that we are children of God" (Rom. 8:16).

A man who meant much to me in my early Christian life was traveling companion to Dr. Donald Grey Barnhouse on one of his many trips to the mission field. He told me that as they made their way across Africa by Land Rover, they came upon a river served by a rather rickety looking ferry, which was the only means of crossing the stream. As they were in midstream, my friend was standing at what passed for a railing. Opposite him was a native boy of about ten or eleven years of age. The boy stared at the man, and the man observed the boy. How could they possibly communicate? Neither one spoke the other's language. My friend had an inspiration. Whistling is not limited by vocabulary. He whistled loudly the music to the first phrase of Robert Lowry's hymn, "What can wash away my sin?" He stopped to see what effect this might have. Immediately the boy whistled back, "Nothing but the blood of Jesus!" Though not a word passed between them, the Holy Spirit had witnessed to the bond between them. They were one in Christ Jesus. A broad smile lit up the boy's face, and the two clasped hands. Some day, before the throne, they will finish the song together.

> What can make me whole again?
>   Nothing but the blood of Jesus.
> Oh! precious is the flow
>   That makes me white as snow;
> No other fount I know,
>   Nothing but the blood of Jesus.

In summary, we have described the unique structure of the Tabernacle as a place worthy of His name—"the place your God shall choose . . . to establish His name there for His dwelling" (Deut. 12:5). The priest could now enter for worship.

The golden walls were seen only by the priests as they entered for worship. God's glory is visible only to the one who comes into His presence to worship, not to the casual spectator.

CHAPTER EIGHT

THE TABLE OF SHEWBREAD

EXODUS 25:23–30

It is the Sabbath day. While activity in the camp is down to a minimum, there is a ceremony specified for this day being carried out at the Tabernacle.

The priests are gathered in a group and standing on the north side of the bronze altar, which is designated as "a holy place" (Lev. 24:9). Eight of them have been appointed for special duties. As the eight appear, four lead the procession empty-handed. The second four follow, two carrying incense bowls and two carrying trays, each holding six newly baked loaves. They enter the Tabernacle, and the four who bring the new loaves and incense bowls take their position on the north side of the table, with those who carry the incense bowls nearest the table. The four who came empty-handed stand on the south side of the table facing their fellows. There must always be fresh bread and incense on this table, so they have come to remove the old and replace them with the new. Those who bring the new loaves and incense make sure that their hands touch the hands of those who remove the loaves and bowls presently on the table, that there may be no gap in the presence of the bread. "And you shall set the bread of the Presence on the table before Me at all times" (Ex. 25:30).[1]

As the group leaves the Holy Place, they carry the two trays with the twelve loaves that have been removed and the two bowls with the incense. The loaves are served to the waiting priests. They pass the loaves from hand to hand, and each one breaks off a piece and passes the remainder to his fellows. Thoughtfully they eat of this bread. It is God's bread, ordered by Him to be kept on this table—"the bread of the Presence" (Ex. 25:30). There was always fresh bread, and always the room was fragrant with the aroma of frankincense as it was sprinkled over the loaves. They cherished this moment each week. God was not renewing but was continuing His presence with them in this real and personal ceremony. The eating of the Presence bread seemed to make God a part of the priests' life as never before.

Between the Sabbaths the table, which stood in the Holy Place, was not involved in the priests' service of worship. Daily they came in to dress the lamps and to put fresh incense on the golden altar. However, as they passed the table, they caught a wisp of fragrance from the frankincense and the lovely smell of bread. There were always twelve loaves, which reminded them of "our twelve tribes" (see Acts 26:7), with whom God had made a solemn and everlasting covenant. The loaves were "the Lord's offerings by fire," and were the priests' "portion forever" (Lev. 24:9). Their continuing presence assured them that Jehovah was present with His people.

Each of the twelve loaves were the same size: "two-tenths of an ephah shall be in each cake" (Lev. 24:5). Thus all were included equally in God's covenant and all received equal blessing, from Benjamin, the smallest tribe, to Judah, the largest.

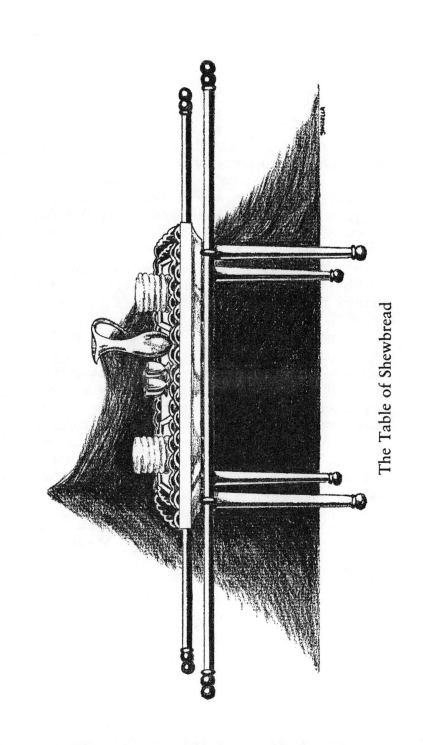

The Table of Shewbread

The table itself took on increased importance as time passed. When first mentioned it was called simply "a table" (Ex. 25:23). Later it was identified as "the table of the bread of the Presence" (Num. 4:7). Though only a table, it became important in the worship of the Tabernacle in that it held "the bread of their God" (Lev. 21:6).

The table was rather small; it was thirty-six inches long by eighteen inches wide by twenty-seven inches high. There were rings at each of the corners and carrying-bars of acacia wood covered with gold, which were provided for transporting the table. Here again we find the acacia wood covered with pure gold, showing us Christ in His humanity and deity. The dimensions of the table made it very stable. God's provision for fellowship with Him is able to withstand all the ordinary jarrings of life.

It is important to notice that God's instructions for the building of the table immediately follow His instructions for the ark and the mercy seat, with no more than the insertion of the word "and." We shall see many things concerning the Holy of Holies, but observe Exodus 25:22–23: "And there I will meet with you, and from above the mercy seat, from between the two cherubim which are upon the ark of the testimony, I will speak to you about all that I will give you in commandment for the sons of Israel. *And* you shall make a table. . . ." (italics mine). God sees all the Tabernacle furniture as equally important. Each piece has its own function and teaches us its own lessons.

Around the top of the table were two golden crown-like borders: one at the edge of the table top and a second a handbreadth (or 4½ inches) outside the other, forming part of a shelf around the top. The twelve loaves or cakes were laid in two rows inside the innermost crown. Since the loaves remained on the table when it was moved from camp to camp, the borders were an extra measure of safety for the bread. The space between the two crowns may well have served as an area for the bowls and implements connected with the frankincense.

We may see our Lord Jesus in the table. We have mentioned the gold of His deity and the acacia wood of His humanity. The two crowns or borders remind us that He was crowned twice during His lifetime. Once the Romans placed a crown of thorns on His head. After the resurrection His Father crowned Him "with glory and honor" (Heb. 2:9). The security given to the loaves by the two crowns should quiet our hearts as we contemplate our own position as we are jostled and jarred in this world around us. With Satan prowling "like a roaring lion", the flesh setting "its desire against the Spirit", and the world keeping up its relentless attacks (see 1 Pet. 5:8; Gal. 5:17), the believer may well be concerned for the safety of his soul. God has prepared for us a double protection against our threefold enemy. In John 10:27–30 the believers are identified as sheep. Two outstanding characteristics of sheep are that they hear and they follow. Believers are not just any sheep; they are "My sheep". "My sheep hear My voice, and I know them, and they follow Me; and I give eternal life to them, and they shall never perish; and no one shall snatch them out of My hand" (vv. 27–28). We have the added assurance that "no one is able to snatch them out of the Father's hand" (v. 29). This is your security, child of God, the two clasped hands of the Father and the Son.

> How firm a foundation,
>   Ye saints of the Lord
> Is laid for your faith
>   In His excellent Word!
> What more can He say
>   Than to you He hath said,

To you who for refuge
To Jesus have fled?
'K' in Rippon's

Selection of Hymns, 1787

As we think further on the loaves, we reflect that a grain of wheat was the beginning of the making of a loaf. It was sowed in the ground, matured, and was reaped. There followed the beating with a flail and the work of the winnowing fan. Then came the grinding between the upper and nether millstones before the sifting process began. There was one sifting screen after another until the flour could be called "fine" (see Lev. 24:5). The next step was preparing the dough with repeated kneadings before it was ready for the baker. Then the loaves were placed in the quick or hot oven as a final step. When properly done, the loaves were removed and carefully placed on the trays ready for the table.

What a wonderful picture of our Lord Jesus is given us here. He identified Himself as the "grain of wheat" (John 12:24) who would fall into the ground, die, and bring forth much fruit. His life and His sufferings were a constant threshing, grinding, and sifting; and the fires of Calvary were the climax. Thus He could plainly say in John 6:51, "I am the living bread that came down out of heaven; if anyone eats of this bread, he shall live forever."

The child of God first encounters this bread when he places his trust in Jesus Christ and receives Him as his personal Savior. In that moment, he is born anew and begins the process of growing in Christ. He comes again to Christ, not for further salvation (that is done once for all), but to learn more about his Lord and the wonderful ways that are mapped out for the Christian. This time of communion is not some miraculous ceremony, nor is it an additional or extraneous experience. The Christian grows by reading and studying the Word of God in order that he may learn more about the Lord Jesus and have a better understanding of God's plan for his life. Perhaps a story from God's Word will help to clarify this point (see Gen. 24).

Abraham and Sarah had a son in their old age. He was truly a miracle child, promised to them by God and born long after the usual time of childbearing for the couple. They named him Isaac, and he became the darling of their lives. Abraham was now old. He lived among pagan idolators, and he dreaded the possibility of his son's marrying into one of those neighboring tribes. He dispatched Eleazar, his eldest servant, on a mission to Mesopotamia, from whence Abraham had come, with instructions to go to Abraham's relatives and select a wife for Isaac. After clarifying the instructions, Eleazar took ten camels, organized a squad of men, and set out on the long journey.

As they neared the city of their destination, Eleazar prayed to Abraham's God that the girl who came from the city and offered to give him a drink of water and to water his camels "be the one whom Thou hast appointed for Thy servant Isaac" (Gen. 24:14). Rebekah appeared on the scene, offered water to Eleazar, and watered his camels. Thus, Eleazar knew that the Lord had guided him to the house of his master's brother.

Eleazar and his men were given lodging in the house. A meal was prepared, but the servant refused to eat until he had told of his mission. He began, "I am Abraham's servant," and proceeded to tell of Abraham's prosperity, power, and prestige and then came to the point of the only son for whom he was charged with obtaining a wife from this city. He pointed out how God had led him to believe that Rebekah was that chosen girl. The family responded,

"The matter comes from the Lord; so we cannot speak to you bad or good" (Gen. 24:50).

Soon Eleazar, Rebekah, and his men were on their way back to Abraham's dwelling. Do you think they rode in silence during the weeks of their camels' plodding? Possibly. But I believe Eleazar recounted the events of Isaac's life, described his height and weight, pictured his face for Rebekah. He spoke of how Isaac's eyes twinkled when he laughed and flashed when he was angry. He told of his gentleness with the flocks and his consideration for the ewes who were with young. Another story dealt with his bravery in defending his flocks from predators. And so, on and on, with each account painting the picture of Rebekah's husband-to-be. Can we not presume that she asked Eleazar again for more details about Isaac? "Did you not say his voice roars when he laughs? And you say his teeth are white as ivory? Tell me again about his eyes twinkling and flashing." Those are natural questions of one about to meet her husband. With each passing mile, Rebekah learned more about her Isaac and longed for the day when she would see him face to face.

How does this loving anticipation apply to the believer?

Among the titles for the church that have come down through the ages, the loveliest is "the bride of Christ." The imagery of those words and the teaching of the Song of Solomon make Rebekah's journey a fitting pattern for the believer as he or she travels through this life to meet the Savior in glory. The Holy Spirit takes us gently by the hand, shows us in God's book the abundance of grace and love we receive from our Lord Jesus, and points out those things that await our meeting Him face to face. It is with light feet that we can walk the paths of earth. Each day finds new wonders for us. His power becomes real. His strength enables us to go through the day. His promises are more precious, and they enable us to speak to others about our wonderful Lord. On some days, the reality of our feeding overwhelms us. We long "to depart and be with Christ" (Phil. 1:23), but He whispers to us, "There is still work to do."

In anticipation of the joy of this feeding, the child of God should make certain that no day goes by without the day's portion from the Word. In this way we are nourished and, above all, provided with strength and wisdom for the tasks that our God has set before us.

As the Israelites journeyed through the wilderness, they were nourished by the manna that fell each day. They gathered this "bread out of heaven" (John 6:32) every day (except the sabbath) for forty years and found their lives sustained and strengthened. Just as the manna was a gift that had to be gathered daily, so is the nourishment that comes from the reading of God's word to be renewed in us each day.

The priests fed on the shewbread, which was the symbol of the everlasting covenant, and indicated that God could be trusted to meet their physical needs. It was not optional for the priests to eat of the bread. It was commanded that they eat (Lev. 24:9). They were to be nourished and strengthened by these loaves.

In the same way, the believer comes to the Word of God daily to learn of Christ and finds Him to be his source of supply, his life, his support, his security and his sanctification for that day. The strength and vigor of our natural life is sustained by each day's food. In today's weight-conscious society, we carefully consider the caloric intake, vitamin content, and balance of protein, carbohydrates, and fats in our diet. Dare we neglect our daily balanced intake of the Word?

At the close of World War II, there were thousands of

G.I.'s and allied troops in prison camps. In addition, there were the survivors in the concentration camps. They had suffered deprivation in nourishment due to unpalatable food and reduced supplies in the lands of their captors. Immediately upon the cessation of hostilities, medical teams were flown in to bring relief. In their supplies were massive doses of vitamin B. Nourishing food was prepared and served, but essential vitamin B was administered to counteract the long periods of undernourishment.

The child of God is no less a captive in this world if that is where he looks for his sustenance. The famished and underfed Christian must have massive intakes of vitamin "B"—Bible, if he is to survive and emerge the victor over this present evil age.

In Psalm 23 David sings of the wonders of his Lord. The climax seems to be in the simple statement, "Thou dost prepare a table before me . . . my cup overflows." Can not our mind's eye see David being nourished at this table? Psalm 145:16 contains David's thanksgiving, "Thou . . . dost satisfy the desire of every living thing."

Believers feed upon the Bread of Life when they gather around the table for communion. That table is usually identified as the communion table, and while in use it holds "the cup of blessing . . . a sharing in the blood of Christ" and "the bread which we break a sharing in the body of Christ" (1 Cor. 10:16). The occasion is identified as the "Lord's Supper." The Holy Spirit, by the apostle Paul, says, "Since there is one bread, we who are many are one body; for we all partake of the one bread" (1 Cor. 10:17).

While most Protestants do not hold the idea that the wine and the bread become the actual blood and body of Christ, there is a call for the Christian to think properly on the occasion. We are a group of believers who have gathered to obey our Lord in doing this "in remembrance of Me" (Luke 22:19). In taking the bread and the cup, we are instructed, "As often as you eat this bread and drink the cup, you proclaim the Lord's death until He comes" (1 Cor. 11:26). The two events listed in this verse (looking back to His death and forward to His coming) are fundamental for the believer. At His death we begin our journey and, unless He delays His coming, we may end our walk with His appearing. In the ceremony it would be entirely fitting if, when the bread is passed, some believer would rise to his feet, hold the morsel of bread aloft, and proclaim, "To Calvary!" The entire company could rise and say with the leader, "To Calvary!" When the cup is passed the toast could be repeated as, "To His soon coming!"

Then the feeding on Christ goes on as each believer reviews in his own thoughts, the steps of his walk from Calvary to the Lord's coming. There is one bread, our Lord Jesus, and we partake of Him daily.

For our encouragement we read, "He has satisfied the thirsty soul, and the hungry soul He has filled with what is good" (Ps. 107:9).

To Jesus every day I find my heart is closer drawn;
   He's fairer than the glory of the gold and purple dawn;
He's all my fancy pictures in its fairest dreams, and more;
   Each day He grows still sweeter than He was the day
      before.

His glory broke upon me when I saw Him from afar;
   He's fairer than the lily, brighter than the morning star;
He fills and satisfies my longing spirit o'er and o'er;
   Each day He grows still sweeter than He was the day
      before.

My heart is sometimes heavy, but He comes with sweet
relief;
He folds me to His bosom when I droop with blighting
grief;
I love the Christ who all my burdens in His body bore;
Each day He grows still sweeter than He was the day
before.

The half cannot be fancied this side the golden shore;
Oh, there He'll be still sweeter than He ever was before.

W. C. Martin

CHAPTER NINE

THE GOLDEN ALTAR OF INCENSE

EXODUS 30:1–10,34–38

"It is most holy to the Lord" (Ex. 30:10). With these words, we take up a study of the golden altar of incense.

The altar occupied a place in the center of the Holy Place just before the veil. It was made of acacia wood covered with pure gold and measured eighteen inches square and thirty-six inches high. The top had a gold molding around it. Horns were added to the top and, while the number is not specified, we may assume that there were four. Two rings, one at each of two opposite corners provided the preparation for traveling by means of two poles of acacia wood covered with gold.

It was at this altar that Aaron, the high priest, burned incense, both morning and evening, as he trimmed the lamps. The acacia and gold again speak of our Lord Jesus in His humanity and deity. It is here that we find His intercessory work as well as the believer's prayer life. We must look with care upon the teaching that is found.

First, the fire for the incense came from the bronze altar where the sacrifice had been consumed (Lev. 16:12–13). Our Lord Jesus entered into His intercessory work based

The Golden Altar of Incense

on His having given Himself as the spotless lamb on the cross. In John 17 we read that He prayed for His own before going to the cross in anticipation of, and in preparation for, the cross. The child of God returns to these precious words time and time again for new nuggets of truth. We read there how He prayed that we might be kept, sanctified, united and glorified. His intercessory work for us continues day by day.

In 1 John 2:1 we have the precious truth that "If anyone sins, we have an Advocate with the Father, Jesus Christ the righteous." The scene before us here is that of the court room. The believer has sinned and Satan, the "accuser of our brethren" (Rev. 12:10), is quick to point out the sin. "See!" he says to God, "there is your Christian. A fine work is he." It is then that our Advocate goes to work. "Father," He says, "this is one for whom I died." We then find that "the blood of Jesus His Son cleanses us from all sin" (1 John 1:7). Here is intercession on a practical level.

> Five bleeding wounds He bears,
>   Received on Calvary;
> They pour effectual prayers,
>   They strongly plead for me;
> "Forgive him, oh, forgive" they cry,
>   "Nor let that ransomed sinner die."
>
> Charles Wesley

How well our Lord knew that we would have need of His intercession! Shortly before His trial and crucifixion, He told Peter, "Satan has demanded permission to sift you like wheat; but I have prayed for you, that your faith may not fail" (Luke 22:31–32). Typically, Peter blurted out a rebuke stating that he was ready to go to prison and death. Our Lord closed the conversation by predicting that Peter would deny Him three times before cock crowing. It is interesting to note that our Lord Jesus did not say He would *keep* Peter from the sifting, but that his faith would not fail *in* the sifting. Before the sifting, Jesus prayed for him. Peter missed this point entirely, but we must not. There comes a day when our faith may be sorely tried. The tempest breaks over our small bark. The waters rage. The wind howls and threatens to sink our craft. Be still my soul! "I have prayed for you." Our plans are fragmented, and we know not where to turn. "I have prayed for you." Darkness rolls over the way before us so that we must grope for that next step. "I have prayed for you." It is "in all these things we overwhelmingly conquer through Him who loved us" (Rom. 8:37).

It was a short time later that Peter warmed himself at the enemy's fire and proceeded to deny his Lord three times. We read, "The Lord turned and looked at Peter" (Luke 22:61). Not a word was spoken, but Peter remembered the Lord's prediction about him, "and he went outside and wept bitterly" (Luke 22:62). Lest we be smug in our self assurance, we need to remember that Jesus has prayed for us before we know of our needs.

In Hebrews 7, we read that after His resurrection Christ became a priest after the order of Melchizedek. This made Him "a priest forever" (Heb. 7:21) who therefore has an unending ministry, since "He always lives to make intercession for them" (Heb. 7:25). The words to emphasize here are "always lives." There is no cessation in His intercession. It is part of His post-resurrection office. Before his crucifixion He prayed for us (see John 17), and He now continues that work. In Psalm 121:4 we read, "Behold, He who keeps Israel will neither slumber nor sleep." How surrounded is the child of God with his Savior's never-failing intercessory, watchful care. This is aptly summarized by Paul Kiene, who writes, "In this, the holy, faithful concern for the total welfare of His own comes to expression. We are totally dependent on the manifold and indispensable ministry of the love of our Lord."[1]

The essential function of the golden altar, was to hold the pot in which the incense was burned. The priest had gathered a firepan full of coals from the bronze altar and had transported them in the incense pot into the Holy Place. There on the golden altar the pure incense was sprinkled on the coals that its fragrance might fill the Holy Place while the priest went about his work of dressing the lamps each morning and evening.

The preparation of the incense was by divine instruction and contained onycha, stacte, galbanum and pure frankincense. Salt was added to prevent deterioration. Israel was forbidden to make this incense for personal use.

The burning of incense is typical of the prayer life of Israel. David's words in Psalm 141:2 are significant: "May my prayer be counted as incense before Thee; the lifting up of my hands as the evening offering." In another example of its use, we read that Zacharias, the father of John the Baptist, "was performing his priestly service before God in the appointed order of his division, [and] according to the custom of the priestly office, he was chosen by lot to enter the temple of the Lord and burn incense. And the whole multitude of the people were in prayer outside at the hour of the incense offering" (Luke 1:8–10). Note here that "the whole multitude" was present for prayer. None were excluded. So also, today, prayer is to be completely natural with every child of God. It is a privilege that should be as normal as breathing. Let there be no hesitancy to bring everything to God.

The basis of prayer has been established at the cross. The conditions of access are through our Lord, who presents our prayers. He entered "heaven itself, now to appear in the presence of God for us" (Heb. 9:24). We also know that no man comes to the Father but by Him (see John 14:6). With this assurance, we should be confident in prayer. It is not a mere exercise but a time of worship in which we commune with our heavenly Father. We speak to Him of our needs, our love, our concerns for a holy life, and the needs and concerns of others. Every part of our daily life can and should be the subject of our prayer. It is through prayer and the study of His Word that we learn how He would order our life, clarify our priorities, direct our feet, open our mouth, and employ our energies.

Not only does Jesus intercede for us before the heavenly throne, we also find that the Holy Spirit is active in our prayer life. He "intercedes for us with groanings too deep for words" and He "intercedes for the saints according to the will of God" (Rom. 8:26–27).

In coming, we come simply. God does not ask for an elaborate or eloquent prayer. He wants to hear a simple, plain, unaffected prayer. Paul tells us that we have received the "spirit of adoption as sons by which we cry out, "Abba! Father!" (Rom. 8:15). These words, "Abba! Father!", are the equivalent of "Daddy." How precious! No human father worries about vocabulary and complete sentences when his small son climbs up onto his lap just to be hugged and perhaps to ask to have a favorite toy mended. The most imperfect sentence finds a listening ear of an earthly father, and so with our Heavenly Father. With both our Lord Jesus and the Holy Spirit praying for us and with us, "Let us therefore draw near with confidence to the throne of grace, that we may receive mercy and find grace to help in time of need" (Heb. 4:16).

We need to take extra care on the one point that might bar the effectiveness of our prayers. Psalm 66:18 warns "If

I regard wickedness in my heart, the Lord will not hear."
Herein lies the great peril to our prayer life. When we
respond to the many encouragements to holy living and a
closer walk with our Lord, we find that we can come to
prayer with a holy boldness knowing that He hears us.

The believers at Ephesus were encouraged to pray for
Paul that "utterance may be given to me in the opening of
my mouth, to make known with boldness the mystery of
the gospel" (Eph. 6:19). While he valued their prayer help,
he sought to broaden their view by exhorting that they "be
on the alert with all perseverance and petition for *all the
saints*"(v. 18, italics mine). This would be sufficient to
challenge the most ardent prayer warrior among them.
Even now there are saints in developing countries who
suffer much for their faith. There are saints in isolated
places who long for some contact with the gospel. There
are saints without the Bible in their own language, who
long for the whole counsel of God. Have you run out of
things to pray for? Try "all the saints," and your prayer list
will have no end.

Twice a day Aaron filled his censer with coals from the
bronze altar, placed incense on the coals, and, with the
fragrant smoke billowing, proceeded into the Holy Place.
There he placed the censer on the golden altar and went
about the work of dressing the lamps. All the while, the
aroma filled the room. When the work was done, he left
the room; but the fragrance of the incense had by that time
permeated his garments. Wherever he went, people knew
that he had been in the Holy Place with the incense.

When our Lord Jesus was here on earth, He spent an
evening at the home of Lazarus, whom He had raised from
the dead. As they reclined at supper, Mary broke the seal
on a pound of very precious spikenard ointment and
anointed the feet of her Lord and wiped His feet with her

hair. We read, "And the house was filled with the fragrance of the ointment" (John 12:3). It is easy to visualize that the fragrance of that poured-out treasure clung to her hair so that for many days anyone with whom she came in contact was reminded of her devotion to her Lord.

As we associate with our friends and co-workers, is there any "sweet aroma" of our having been in the secret place with our God? In reality, there can be no such thing as a "secret believer." Our walk with God, our feeding on His Word, our time spent in prayer must cling to our very being for all to know. Aaron could no more brush away the odor of the incense from his garments nor Mary comb from her hair that perfume of the spikenard, than can we emerge from a time of prayer without some heavenly fragrance showing itself to those around us. Paul, in writing to the believers at Corinth, says that "God . . . manifests through us the sweet aroma of the knowledge of Him in every place. For we are a fragrance of Christ to God among those who are being saved and among those who are perishing" (2 Cor. 2:14–15).

Lest we fall into the trap of requiring some ecstatic experience at every time of prayer, let us remember that "even the feeblest expression or exhibition of Him, in the life or worship of a saint, is an odor of a sweet smell in which God is well pleased."[2]

Prayer is not only a fragrance, it is a power. Our twentieth century houses are wired for electricity. In every room, we find switches and outlets which are connected to a main switch panel. Every house, in turn, is connected through a network to a power plant which is fueled by coal, oil, or even nuclear energy to run the generators. From these plants the power is fed to our homes and to industry. With such resources available, it would be foolish for us to go about our lives by candlelight, groping and limiting our lives by the small circle of the light which the candle supplies. With kilowatts at our command, why should we rely on candles? Turn on a switch; plug in a lamp! Too many Christians live a "candle life" when God's kilowatts are to be had. Plug your life into God through prayer and intercession.

In Acts 6 we read of the problem of the early church in caring for their needy. The twelve disciples suggested to the assembly that men should be sought out to take care of this phase of the ministry and, they added, "We will devote ourselves to prayer, and to the ministry of the word" (Acts 6:4). Note the verb, "devote." Among its meanings is, "to addict." This activity of devotion sets the tone for the place of prayer in the believer's life. It becomes a necessity for daily living, a part of our lives that controls our whole being. Our spiritual life is vigorous and growing to the degree that prayer draws us irresistibly to our Savior's throne for each day's need.

Come, my soul, thy suit prepare;
  Jesus loves to answer prayer;
He Himself has bid thee pray,
  Therefore will not say thee nay.

Thou art coming to a King;
  Large petitions with thee bring;
For His grace and power are such,
  None can ever ask too much.

With my burden, I begin—
  Lord, remove this load of sin;
Let Thy blood, for sinners spilt,
  Set my conscience free from guilt.

Lord, I come to Thee for rest—
  Take possession of my breast,

There Thy blood-bought right maintain,
  And without a rival reign.

While I am a pilgrim here
  Let Thy love my spirit cheer;
As my Guide, my Guard, my Friend,
  Lead me to my journey's end.

Show me what I have to do,
  Every hour my strength renew;
Let me live a life of faith,
  Let me die Thy people's death.

John Newton

CHAPTER TEN

THE GOLDEN LAMPSTAND
EXODUS 25:31–40; 27:20–21; 37:17–24

"God is light, and in Him there is no darkness at all"
(1 John 1:5). As we turn to the south side of the
Holy Place, a remarkable sight meets our eyes—a lampstand of pure gold, holding seven lamps set ablaze with
coals from the bronze altar. It furnishes illumination for
the believer-priest as he eats at the table of shewbread and
prays and intercedes at the golden altar of incense.

The lampstand was a piece of exquisite gold work and
reflected Bezalel's spirit-filled craftsmanship. No dimensions are given, but we can be sure that it stood higher than
the table and the altar, possibly six feet. It was of one piece
beaten out of one lump of pure gold. Thousands of hammer blows were rained upon it, as the shaft and six
branches took the shape of the likeness of the almond
tree's bud, blossom and fruit. The almond tree is called the
awakening tree or the vigilant tree throughout the East,
where it is the first tree to flower after the winter, sometimes bursting into bloom as early as January. The almond
decoration points to the resurrection of Christ. Let us
remember that in the test with the leaders of the tribes, it
was Aaron's rod that "sprouted and put forth buds and

produced blossoms, and it bore ripe almonds," showing God's ability to bring life out of death (Num. 17:8).

The gold speaks to us of Christ in His glory, and the lack of dimensions says that His glory is immeasurable.

Gold cannot be bruised or destroyed by hammering. In the hands of a skilled workman, such as Bezalel or Oholiab, the gold would be stretched, formed, and beautified. The process of beaten work reminds us of Christ's sufferings as the blows fell upon Him. The first of these strokes came upon Him soon after His birth when His parents fled into Egypt to escape Herod's decree (see Matt. 2:13–15). He was rejected by His own brothers and sisters (see Ps. 69:8). He suffered at the hands of His own countrymen and in His hometown so that "He could do no miracle there. . . . He wondered at their unbelief" (Mark 6:5–6). The religious leaders rose against Him (see Matt. 12:14). Satan attacked Him with temptations (see Matt. 4:1–2) and throughout His life he sought to destroy Him. All of these attacks were from the world and Satan, but the crowning blow came on the cross when He was made sin for us and God turned His back on His Son (see 2 Cor. 5:21; Mark 15:34). So must the lives of believers be changed by the hammer blows of love to let His divine glory shine out from us (see Matt. 5:16).

The center shaft of the lampstand is typical of our Lord Jesus's centrality: He occupied the center cross with a criminal on either side (see John 19:18); He is in the midst of His servants in heaven (see Rev. 7:15; 22:3); He is preeminent in creation (see Col. 1:18), the "outstanding among ten thousand" (see Song 5:10).

The six branches of the lampstand came out from the shaft in three pairs one above another. Since the lampstand is a picture of the person and work of the Lord Jesus, these six branches may portray the six aspects of the Holy

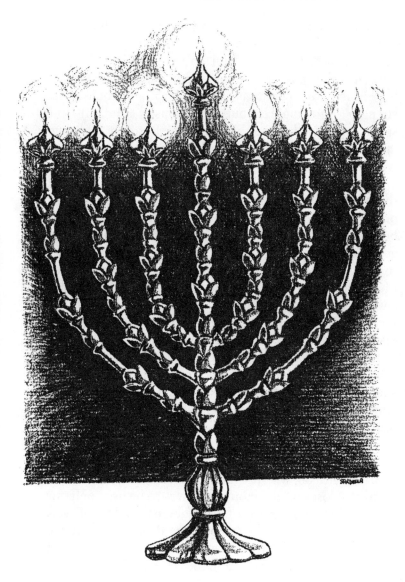

The Golden Lampstand

Spirit's work in Christ. In Isaiah 11, we see Him as the "shoot . . . from the stem of Jesse" (v. 1) who has the Spirit of the Lord resting upon Him. In the three branches, we have (1) "the spirit of wisdom and understanding" showing His inward commitment, (2) "the spirit of counsel and strength" showing His outward ministry, and (3) "the spirit of knowledge and the fear of the Lord" (v. 2) bringing to us His communion with His heavenly Father. Thus was He prepared to do and speak for God the Father.

The believer-priest should never lose sight of the fact that the same anointing of the Holy Spirit that descended on Jesus (see Matt. 3:16) now rests on the church, His body (see 1 Cor. 12:13). That Spirit enables us to know, to act, and to speak in His name. The Holy Spirit brings gifts to every believer: first, to give knowledge for a Spirit-filled life; second, to enable us to act upon the knowledge gained; and third, to communicate the good news. We know more than we do. When God speaks to us, our response falls far short of the enablement He has provided.

There were seven lamps, one of which rested on the end of each of the branches and the central shaft. These were again of pure gold beaten work and may speak of the Holy Spirit. The number seven points us to divine perfection (see Rev. 4:5). The lamps were filled with pure olive oil, the result of crushing olives in a mortar and pestle. (In the crushing, Christ's sufferings are again portrayed; see Is. 53:10.) This oil was prepared according to instructions given to Moses on the mount and was to be used only for the worship and service of the Tabernacle. The oil was renewed daily when the lamps were dressed so that the light from the lamps would never go out. Each lamp had a wick which carried the oil from the vessel to the flame. The oil shows us the moving of the Holy Spirit, and the wick can be no other than the believer himself "baptized" into the one body by the Holy Spirit (see 1 Cor. 12:13) and set afire by God that he might be a light for God.

In the course of burning, the wicks would become charred and burned down. Both the charring and the shortening were taken care of when the priests trimmed the lamps at evening. The charred portion was snipped off, and the wick was adjusted so that the oil could flow freshly and the flame would burn brightly. The snipped-off ends were not carelessly discarded but were carefully collected in a snuff dish. God remembers these trimmings as He does our tears, which are in His bottle and His book (see Ps. 56:8).

As we walk day by day, mere contact with the world brings sin into our lives. Even as we minister for God there may be pride or, even worse, a false humility that comes from an unexpected, positive response to the teaching of the Word. These charrings of our wick need to be dealt with. The sin must be "snipped off", and the wick cleansed and lifted. Likewise, the sin of pride must be confessed and put away. As the lamps were trimmed daily, so must we daily examine our walk by the Holy Spirit and deal firmly with the sin that has shown itself. Failure to do this will make for more smoke and smell than shining, and we shall miss the whole purpose of the Holy Spirit's presence within us. Judson Cornwall has an excellent paragraph on this point.

> The Spirit comes to him (the believer), the fire comes upon him, and the oil flows through him. But unless the wick of that humanity is kept in right relationship between the oil and the fire, there will be far more smell and smoke than light. If pride elevates the wick too high, the flame will not burn correctly; too much smoke. If self-depreciation causes the wick to lower itself too low it will either extinguish the flame or cause it to burn so impurely that more odor than light is produced. But smoke, stink and soot are

eliminated when the wick is properly and regularly trimmed and adjusted.[1]

The purpose of the lampstand was to provide light for the Holy Place. Remember that there were no windows in the Tabernacle; so no natural light was let in. The priests were not permitted to carry a lamp in from outside. No ordinary light was allowed. There was only the light of the seven lamps on the lampstand as they remained filled and trimmed and burning.

The light shone first on the lampstand, illuminating itself. How perfect a picture of the Holy Spirit carrying out His duty of glorifying Christ, as He takes the things of Christ and shows them to us (see John 16:14). Then the rays fell on the table of shewbread and gave light as the priests fulfilled their privilege of eating the bread at the end of each week. As we look to our Lord in the pages of His book, thereby partaking of the Bread of Life, and as we think on the things we find, we are grateful to have the Holy Spirit illuminating our worship. As the circle of light expands, we see the altar of incense and find again that our praying and interceding must be guided by the Holy Spirit (see Rom. 8. 26–27). It is important that we be in the Spirit as we pray, lest we slip into "vain repetitions" and our interceding fail to rise above our heads. God has provided through His Holy Spirit that we neither labor nor pray in vain.

The golden walls reflected the light from the lampstand, and in this we may see our Lord Jesus as the lampstand, serving to highlight the glory of the Father.

The curtain hangings, which formed the ceiling of the Holy Place, also received light from the lampstand. The veil, too, which sealed off the most Holy Place, was shone upon by the lamps. The cherubim woven into these two hangings with colors of blue, purple, and scarlet were made radiant by the light of the lamps. These guardians of the holiness of God remind today's believer-priest that his fellowship at the table, his prayer life at the altar, and his life as a shining witness for God are all to be carried out in the light of the holiness of God.

One final but solemn thought: the more the lamps burn, the more they must be trimmed. The more God is pleased to use us, and the closer He would have us walk with Him, the more we will need His hand to trim and adjust our lives for Him. The lamps were intended only to give light, and they performed an important function of illuminating the work of the priest. Let us be sure that we are faithful in this very fundamental task.

The lampstand was placed in the Holy Place and could not be seen by outsiders. It was only when the priest went into the Holy Place that he saw the lampstand and worshiped in its light. The world around us may speculate as to Christ and His mission, perhaps calling Him the Great Teacher, a Perfect Man, or an Example; but only the believer-priest knows the real glory of God in the face of Jesus Christ (see 2 Cor. 4:6) when he goes into the Holy Place to minister. Christ is the light—not to the world but *to* His people (see 1 John 1:7), *in* His people (see 2 Cor. 4:6) and *through* His people (Matt. 5:16).

When Bezalel started work on the lampstand, he looked upon the lump of pure gold and visualized the finished product in all its grace and beauty. God, too, looks upon us as sinners to be transformed by the work of Christ until He marks us "holy and blameless before Him. In love He predestined us to adoption as sons through Jesus Christ to Himself, according to the kind intention of His will, to the praise of the glory of His grace, which He freely bestowed on us in the Beloved" (Eph. 1:4–6).

The instructions for the making of the lampstand are accompanied by an extra warning not given to any other part of the Tabernacle. The builder of the lamps and the stand, is exhorted with this added word: "And see that you make them after the pattern for them, which was shown to you on the mountain" (Ex. 25:40). God's lightbearer must be of God's design.

CHAPTER ELEVEN

THE VEIL

EXODUS 26:31–37

The young apprentice-priest had anticipated this day for a long time. Many months and years of study and training were coming to an end. Now he was to be anointed and robed, having the blood and oil placed on his right ear, his right thumb and the great toe of his right foot. He was to be assigned to one of the ranks of priests who would carry out the prescribed worship functions. It was an important day!

Among other things, he would make his first visit to the Holy Place. He imagined drawing aside the screen of the doorway and stepping inside. Coming in from the bright sunlight, his eyes would require a few moments to adjust to the lamplight. The room would glow as the light from the lampstand revealed the table, the altar of incense, the beautiful ceiling, and the golden walls. As his eyes moved from the furniture, the walls, and the ceiling, his gaze would become fixed on the drapery at the end of the room. There it would be—the veil! From side to side his eyes would trace its pattern, the magnificent background with the figures of the cherubim embroidered in blue, scarlet, and purple on the white byssus. Those figures of cherubim would remind him of their function as guardians of the holiness of God, and he trembled with excitement and awe. However, he realized that this Holy Place, with all its beauty, was as far as he might go—unless, that is, unless he should one day become the high priest. He knew that the only person to pass beyond the veil was the high priest, and even he could only do so once a year; and for that he had to go through an awesome ceremony, offer sacrifices, wear special clothing, and take blood and incense with him.

The apprentice might have wondered at the fact that only one tribe lived around the Tabernacle; only one family attended to the ceremonies of the Holy Place, and only one man once a year could pass beyond the veil. As far as he, the apprentice, was concerned, the beautiful veil was a barrier to keep him as well as the other priests out of the presence of God, who dwelt between the cherubim and above the mercy seat. Beautiful as it might have been, the veil bade him stop. He could go no farther.

The veil was suspended from four pillars of acacia wood overlaid with gold (see Ex. 26:32). The pillars were fitted into bases of silver. The pillars again speak of Christ's humanity and deity; the bases or sockets of silver point to Christ our Redeemer (see 1 Cor. 1:30). Strangely enough, there is no mention of a capital or decorative top for these four pillars (compare Ex. 27:10; 36:38). This lack of architectural completeness stands out in contrast to the minute detail of the other instructions. This "unfinished" description reminds us that "He was cut off out of the land of the living" (Is. 53:8).

The four pillars (contrasted with five for the gate) held up the veil. Since the veil represents the person of our Lord, we are reminded of the four gospel writers—Matthew, Mark, Luke, and John—who present the four portraits of

Christ. Matthew depicts His kingship; Mark emphasizes His role as servant; Luke portrays Him as Son of Man; and John sets forth His Godhead. Christ has also given four gifts to His believers: wisdom, righteousness, santification, and redemption (see 1 Cor. 1:30).

The veil is one of the types of Christ about which there can be no question as to its meaning. Hebrews 10:19–22 clearly states,

Since therefore, brethren, we have confidence to enter the holy place by the blood of Jesus, by a new and living way which He inaugurated for us through *the veil, that is, His flesh*, and since we have a great priest over the house of God, let us draw near with a sincere heart in full assurance of faith, having our hearts sprinkled clean from an evil conscience and our bodies washed with pure water [italics mine].

"The veil, that is, His flesh"—as we contemplate this fact, we come face to face with the knowledge that God invaded history and was "made in the likeness of men" (Phil. 2:7). Hebrews 2:9 tells us that He "has been made for a little while lower than the angels . . . because of the suffering of death." This mission of God's Son was no last minute rescue effort but was in the mind of God from the beginning. Peter tells us that He "was foreknown before the foundation of the world" (1 Pet. 1:20). Paul speaks of "the eternal purpose" of God (see Eph. 3:11) and the "purpose and grace which was granted us in Christ Jesus from all eternity" (2 Tim. 1:9). Paul also makes the point to Titus that "eternal life . . . [was] promised long ages ago" by God (Titus 1:2). Paul makes one grand statement on the coming of Christ which serves to put this enormous event into perspective. "Great is the mystery of godliness:"

He who was revealed in the flesh,
Was vindicated in the Spirit,
Beheld by angels,
Proclaimed among the nations,
Believed on in the world,
Taken up in glory
(1 Tim. 3:16).

In one sentence he sums up the coming, ministry, death, resurrection, ascension, and proclamation of our Lord. I fear that the world and Satan have so succeeded in infiltrating our observance of Christmas that the true majesty of the incarnation is lost sight of. The manger of Bethlehem held none other than the Creator of heaven and earth who had come on a very specific mission.

The theme of the Epistle to the Hebrews is—*Christ, greater than.* In chapter 1, we read that He is greater than angels; in chapter 3, He is declared greater than Moses; in chapters 6 and 7, we see Him as greater than the Levitical priesthood, being a priest after the order of Melchizedek with an ever-living priesthood. Chapter 10 shows Him as greater than the Levitical sacrifices.

The tenth chapter of Hebrews is one of the mountain peaks of Scripture. We traverse its content over many intermediate valleys and heights, with each ascent bringing a breathtaking view of the valley beyond and the greater height to come. The climb begins at verse 1, where the writer makes the point that, wonderful as they were, the Old Testament sacrifices were only a shadow of the good things to come and that these sacrifices, though offered year by year, could never make those perfect who drew near. He then points out that Jesus came to do the will of God and, to accomplish this, He took on a body "prepared for Me" (Heb. 10:5). Jesus is quoted as saying that burnt offerings and sacrifices for sin were not really what God had desired, although He had ordered them. They were but a shadow, and the plan had always been that He, Jesus, would come to take away the shadow and establish the substance. This is done "through the offering of the body of Jesus Christ once for all" (Heb. 10:10).

As we study and meditate in this tenth chapter of Hebrews, a series of vivid contrasts present themselves showing the difference between the sacrifices of the law and that of our Lord Jesus:

Sacrifices of the Law		Sacrifices of Christ	
According to the law	v.8	According to the will of God	v.7
Shadow of good things to come	v.1	*Form* of things to come	v.1
Same sacrifices offered year by year continually	v.1	One sacrifice offered once	vv.12,14
Never ceased	v.2	Once for all	v.10
Priest stands daily offering same sacrifices	v.11	Christ offered one sacrifice and sat down	v.12
God took no pleasure in them	v.6	God accepted the sacrifice	vv.5,7
Impossible to take away sins	v.4	Took away sins once for all	v.10
Can never make perfect or take away sins	vv.1,11	By one offering He has perfected for all time those who are sanctified	v.14
Reminder of sins every year	v.3	God will remember sins no more	v.17

The boy Jesus, "the holy offspring" (Luke 1:35), grew and became "strong, increasing in wisdom; and the grace of God was upon Him" (Luke 2:40). At twelve he had to be in His Father's house (see Luke 2:49). In His manhood He withstood the testing of Satan (see Luke 4:4,8,12) and the blandishments of those who would make Him king before the appointed time (see John 6:15). Before the religious authorities, He flung down the challenge, "Which one of you convicts Me of sin?" (John 8:46). There was no reply. In His trial, He gained the positive testimony of Pilate—"I find no guilt in Him" (John 19:4)—and in His death the praise statement of the centurion—"Certainly this man was innocent" (Luke 23:47). All those incidents underscored His spotless humanity and qualified Him to become the Lamb of God (see John 1:29). This personal holiness of our Lord has been acknowledged and admired over the ages even by those who would rank Him only as a great teacher or a challenging example.

In the beauty of the veil, we see two things. First, only in this lovely drapery is the order of the colors changed. Usually the reference to color, whether woven or embroidered, is white linen (byssus), blue, scarlet, and purple. In that order, the spotless humanity is emphasized in the linen with the added reference in the other colors to His heavenly origin, His work as the suffering servant, and His royal lineage. But here in the veil, as though to challenge those who see only the holy humanity, the color blue is mentioned first to underscore His heavenly origin. Indications are that the color blue predominated in the veil, with the figures of cherubim worked out in the white, scarlet, and purple. The veil shows us Emmanuel, "God with us", who has been "made for a little while lower than the angels . . . because of the suffering of death crowned with glory and honor" (Heb. 2:9). Second, lovely as the veil might have been, it was still a barrier. It kept Israel at a distance. The unrepentant man had three barriers between him and God: the gate, the door, and the veil. The sinning but repentant man could come and pass through the gate with the proper sacrifice, but could go no farther than the bronze altar. The priest could turn from his work at the bronze altar, wash at the laver, and pass through the screen of the door. Once inside the Holy Place, he could burn incense and pray at the golden altar, commune at the table, all the while having his worship and his steps illuminated by the light of the lampstand. But to go farther was the sole, overwhelming duty and privilege of the high priest once a year. At all other times it was a barrier to him as well as to the priests of lesser office. The beautiful veil was an effective barrier.

Admiration for the beauty of the veil did not make entrance possible, but the sprinkling of atoning blood before the veil did. That was the only way of passing beyond the veil. It was the sprinkling of the blood before the veil and the carrying of the blood of the victim beyond it. It was blood of substitution for a sinner who acknowledged his need. Similarly, the spotless humanity of Jesus, much as we would admire it and attempt an imitation, could not bring us to God. Faith in His blood, shed for us, gives us confidence to enter. As the rent veil made the way open to the sinner, the rent body of our Lord Jesus (His flesh) gives us entrance to His presence.

Three crosses stood starkly against the sky that formed the backdrop for a hill called Golgotha, the place of a skull. On the center cross, the Son of God was giving His life as a ransom for many. Here was dying "the just for the unjust, in order that He might bring us to God" (1 Pet. 3:18). As the day wore on, the spectacle moved some to taunting, some to weeping, some to quarreling over His clothing, and some to repentance. We read, "And about the ninth hour Jesus cried out with a loud voice, saying, 'Eli, Eli, Lama sabacthani?' that is, 'My God, My God, why hast Thou forsaken Me?'" (Matt. 27:46). His sin-bearing had become an awesome burden. A short time later He shouted, "Finished," and "handed over His Spirit" (John 19:30, author's paraphrase). Then follows the tremendous statement, "And behold, the veil of the temple was torn in two from top to bottom" (Matt. 27:51). The barrier that had stood in the way for centuries was now gone. The rent "veil of His flesh" was now a highway of grace.

The sinner had been shut out from God, but now he has access or "introduction by faith into this grace in which we stand; and we exult in hope of the glory of God" (Rom. 5:2). We have a great high priest in our Lord Jesus who has gone beyond the veil into heaven itself for us. "Not through the blood of goats and calves, but through His own blood, He entered the holy place once for all, having obtained eternal redemption" (Heb. 9:12). Having done this He has opened the way for us to enter—". . . therefore, brethren, we have confidence to enter the holy place by the blood of Jesus, by a new and living way which He inaugurated for us through the veil, that is, His flesh" (Heb. 10:19–20).

The rending of the veil, as set forth in the Gospels, is of great importance and blessing to us as we compare the details with the events set forth in Hebrews 10.

From the Matthew account, it is clear that the rending of the veil in the temple was simultaneous with the death of Christ. For many years the veil had hung suspended in the temple. Now with the cataclysmic event at Calvary, the veil "was torn in two from top to bottom" (Matt. 27:51). Our Lord Jesus was suspended between heaven and earth when He was struck by the hand of God. The fact that the veil was torn from top to bottom tells us that the same hand that had made the tear had put His Son to grief (see Is. 53:10; Ps. 38:2, 42:7). This was a complete tear, just as Christ's work on Calvary was complete. There is nothing for us to do. We cannot add to it in any way. Luke 23:45 implies that the tear was in the middle, thereby exposing the ark and the mercy seat. Any person claiming Christ as Savior may now come directly to Him. There is no need for anyone to take a side entrance or any roundabout way. You may now come directly to God through Christ without any hesitation.

The following words from Donald Grey Barnhouse's book, *God's River*, eloquently sum up the teaching of the rent veil:

> The veil has been torn away, the way is open. We need not approach God as cringing creatures, afraid of the shadow of our sin. We do not have to hang back like rebels before an offended monarch. We do not hesitate in fear because of the pollution of our Adam's natures. The veil has been torn in two. We come with holy boldness. We need no intercessor other than Christ.
>
> There is a simple story about Abraham Lincoln as an illustration of what we have a right to expect. A southern soldier, who had been freed from prison camp because he was wounded too sorely to return to active duty, was seeking access to the President in order to intercede for his brother, the sole support of their mother, who was then in a prison camp. The soldiers on guard at the White House would not let him in. One day a little Tad Lincoln, the President's son, was walking near the White House, he observed the crippled veteran seated on a bench crying. The boy asked what the matter was. The man explained that he wanted to see Mr. Lincoln to tell about his brother, but the soldiers would not let him in. Tad took the man by

the hand and led him past the guards into the presence of his father. When I was desolate and alone, wounded by sin and mourning my lost state, the Son of God came from Heaven, died to pay the debt of my sin, and was raised from the dead in order that He might take me by the hand and lead me to His throne, past angel guards that have barred the way, and in spite of the forces of the enemy of souls who would love to keep me from the place of comfort and blessing. The Son of God is my access into the grace where I now stand, and I need not any of the others for whom He died. I need only Jesus, and praise God, I have Jesus—the Lord Jesus Christ—my Jesus.[1]

In the veil we see God's grace in removing any barrier in the way of our coming to Him through Christ. Let us make haste to enter in.

CHAPTER TWELVE

THE ARK

EXODUS 25:10–16; 37:1–5

We pass now through the torn veil into the Holy of Holies and look upon the furniture within—the ark and its accompanying cover, the mercy seat. The room is a perfect cube, being fifteen feet in all directions. This gives an air of perfection to all that shall be seen. The veil fills the entrance side of the room. The other three walls are made of the gold covered boards with the two corner boards of special design as we saw in Chapter 7. The ceiling is a continuation of the innermost drapery of linen, with cherubim embroidered throughout in scarlet, blue, and purple. The floor is the desert sand.

Without question, the ark was the focal point of the entire Tabernacle. It was a modest piece of furniture, being forty-five inches long by twenty-seven inches high and twenty-seven inches wide. It was made of the now familiar acacia wood covered with gold, but note that this piece was covered or overlaid with gold both inside *and* outside. There was no wood showing. We shall see that it sets forth our Lord Jesus in quite a different way from all that has gone before. The absence of visible wood would draw attention to His deity; therefore, as we move along in our examination, the divine person will be foremost in our minds rather than some aspect of His work.

Though He took "the form of a bond-servant, and [was] made in the likeness of men"; yet we are not to forget that "He existed in the form of God, [and] did not regard equality with God a thing to be grasped" (Phil. 2:6,7). In Proverbs 9:10 we read, "the fear of the Lord is the beginning of wisdom, and the knowledge of the Holy One is understanding." Isaiah wrote the following words, "For thus says the high and exalted One . . . 'I dwell on a high and holy place, and also with the contrite and lowly of spirit'" (Is. 57:15). "Equality with God," "the Holy One," "the high and exalted One"—these phrases all serve to emphasize our Lord's exalted deity. While we humans now have access into the Holiest by the blood of Jesus, this ease of access in no way lessens the deity of our Lord. We are invited into the throne room of the Lord Jehovah, but it is only through His matchless grace that we are allowed to enter. How shall we come? The priests wore no sandals or shoes as they ministered in the Tabernacle and later in the Temple. Perhaps you have seen the peoples of the Orient put aside their shoes as they enter their temples and mosques for worship. This is a fitting act of reverence. When we remember that Moses received his commission from God with unclad feet, our approach to the Holiest should be, like these outward signs, with proper humility.

Moses was a changed person after his first meeting with Jehovah. Similarly, once we have met our Lord at the cross, the natural yearning of our hearts should be to walk in His presence. As we pour out our hearts in petition and adoration and He speaks to us by His Holy Spirit from His Word, such intercourse must have a lasting effect on our lives. Paul writes these wonderful words, "For God, who said, 'Light shall shine out of darkness,' is the One who has shone in our hearts to give the light of the knowledge of the glory of God in the face of Christ" (2 Cor. 4:6). God has shone in our hearts that our lives might reflect that light to others.

The room, "the Holiest," contained the throne of God; and the ark was an essential part of that throne. The altar of incense, the lampstand, and the table of shewbread were called "holy"; but they were on the other side of the veil. The ark and the mercy seat alone were within the veil. Geoffrey Bull writes, "In the Holiest Place there is no place for Holy things but only for the Holy One".[1] It is the Lord Jesus Christ Himself in all His majestic deity that we encounter in the ark.

The importance of the ark is emphasized by the fact that the term appears some 180 times throughout Scripture. Its names are indicative of its function as well as its value:

The ark of the covenant of the Lord of all
the earth (Josh. 3:11)
The ark of the testimony (Ex. 25:22)
The holy ark (2 Chr. 35:3)
The ark of Thy strength (Ps. 132:8)
The ark of the covenant of the Lord (Num. 10:33)
The ark of God (1 Sam. 3:3)
The ark of the Lord God (1 Kin. 2:26)

The children of Israel spent some forty years in the wilderness before reaching their land of promise. Although it may seem that they were lost, they were not. In fact they had an infallible guide. We read, "Whenever the cloud was lifted from over the tent, afterward the sons of Israel would then set out; and in the place where the cloud settled down, there the sons of Israel would camp. At the command of the Lord the sons of Israel would set out, and

The Ark of the Covenant

at the command of the Lord they would camp" (Num. 9:17–18).

The ark was ready to be moved at any time. The carrying poles were left in the four golden rings (see Ex. 25:15). A blast from the two silver trumpets was the signal to strike camp (see Num. 10:1f.). The priests entered the Tabernacle, took down the veil, and wrapped it around the ark. The other items were wrapped and protected. It was God, whose presence was represented in the ark and the cloud pillar, who headed the procession and searched out a resting place for them: "They set out from the mount of the Lord three days' journey, with the ark of the covenant of the Lord journeying in front of them for the three days, to seek out a resting place for them" (Num. 10:33). Would that we would move only "at the command of the Lord."

How beautifully this reminds us of our Lord Jesus's words about His sheep—"When he puts forth all His own, he goes before them, and the sheep follow him because they know his voice" (John 10:4). These words speak of obedient sheep, but, unfortunately, all sheep are not that way. Unlike David's description of the "sheep of Thy pasture" (Ps. 79:13), Isaiah paints a picture of "sheep . . . gone astray. Each of us has turned to his own way" (Is. 53:6). In his delightful book on the twenty-third psalm, Phillip Keller tells us how sheep must be constantly cared for. They have to be led. Fresh pastures must be found; disease must be fended off; shady places of rest are necessary; cool, fresh water must be provided. All of these tasks require a diligent, alert, and, above all, loving shepherd. If the shepherd relaxes for one moment, the sheep will stupidly and blindly follow old trails until the food is gone, drink of polluted streams, and wander aimlessly until they are lost.[2] But our Good Shepherd, that Great Shepherd, goes before us when He sends us forth. In the

Amplified Old Testament the last verse of Psalm 23 reads, "I will dwell in the presence of the Lord forever." In the Holiest, we are before the throne of God and in the presence of the Lord. Where He leads us out, let us follow. He leads us to the green pastures for food, the crystal flowing streams for refreshing drink, the quiet cool spot for rest. He can see us through times of doubt and despair. Just to know that "He goes before" will encourage us to take that step onto unknown ground. God has led His believing saints for centuries, and He is just the same today.

The ark represented God's presence with Israel in battle (1 Sam. 4:3–4) and accompanied them as they moved into the land, which was new and strange territory to them. It is vital for the believer to remember that he is a pilgrim in a hostile land. As he encounters the forces of the enemy of souls, he is warned by James, "Submit therefore to God. Resist the devil and he will flee from you" (James 4:7). (Note well that the submitting comes *before* the resisting.) It is not a strange thing for the child of God to meet opposition. Israel was moving in to dispossess established peoples who were not prepared to hand over their lands meekly. Israel had to fight. Satan will resist your witness for Christ and do anything to prevent one of his from responding to the gospel. But as the ark showed God's leadership in battle, so will and does our God lead us today. He is our strength when we meet Satan, the flesh, and the world. "The weapons of our warfare are not of the flesh" (2 Cor. 10:4). Thus could Nehemiah, in his preparations to defend the rebuilding of the wall of Jerusalem, encourage his band by telling them that "Our God will fight for us" (Neh. 4:20).

The second verse of Martin Luther's "A Mighty Fortress" reads,

Did we in our own strength confide,
   Our striving would be losing;
Were not the right Man on our side,
   The Man of God's own choosing:
Dost ask who that may be?
   Christ Jesus, it is He;
Lord Sabaoth, His name,
   From age to age the same,
And He must win the battle.

As the people of Israel marched or camped, they were very much aware of the fact that God was also walking and communing with them. God spoke to Moses "as a man speaks to his friend" (Ex. 33:11). In the special promises to Israel, we have these words, "Moreover, I will make My dwelling among you, and My soul will not reject you. I will also walk among you and be your God, and you shall be My people" (Lev. 26:11–12). Today the child of God has these precious words for himself. "If we walk in the light as He Himself is in the light, we have fellowship with one another" (1 John 1:7). God is in the midst of His people even today. We miss much if we fail to recognize this and know this fellowship and its effects day by day.

Moses, on the mount, received the Ten Commandments, the design of the Tabernacle and its furnishings, and instruction from God about many things. When he came out to pass on the instructions to the people, they noticed an unusual glow on his face. It so distracted them and partly terrified them that, as he was ready to transfer to them the instructions received, he would place a veil over his face. When he went back for further communion with Jehovah, he took off the veil. It is our privilege to walk in the light with the same God who walked with Moses. As we speak with our blessed Lord and He speaks to us, is there a glow from that exchange that those around us can see? May our hearts be exercised to make this fellowship real day by day!

The ark is the only piece of furniture here which functions as the base for another. In the ark, or the base, we see the Son of God in His deity. In the mercy seat, which sits on top of it, we find the place of propitiation, (as we shall see later) where the evidence for the sacrificial offering is set forth—in the blood of the Son of God, the Savior. We have seen these two aspects of our Lord's life and death before, but the combining of them in the ark serves to underscore the fact that it is "God *our Savior*" who occupies the throne. In his letters to Timothy and Titus, Paul speaks of "God our Savior" (see 1 Tim. 1:1; 2:3; 4:10; Titus 1:3,4; 2:10). Peter and Jude repeat this title (see 2 Pet. 1:1; Jude 25). It is God Himself "who loved me, and delivered Himself up for me" (Gal. 2:20).

The decorative crown or molding around the top of the ark is a further use of the crowns as found in the table of shewbread and the golden altar of incense, where the deity of our Lord is emphasized. The crown of the ark held the mercy seat securely and served to finish off the symmetry of the structure. For a throne room, this crown for our Lord is most fitting. The Magi came seeking Him who was "born King of the Jews" (Matt. 2:2). The soldiers mockingly hailed Him as "King of the Jews" (Matt. 27:29) and crowned Him with a circlet of thorns. Pilate recognized majesty in Him and to the people said, "Behold, your King!" (John 19:14). The real coronation came from God the Father who "highly exalted Him" (Phil. 2:9) and crowned Him "with glory and honor" (Heb. 2:9). Finally we see Him at the right hand of the Father with "many diadems" (Rev. 19:12). One day we shall join with that great throng in glory who "cast their crowns before the throne" (Rev. 4:10). "Worthy is the Lamb that was slain to receive power and riches and wisdom and might and honor and glory and blessing" (Rev. 5:12). Even today, He deserves the first place in our lives and will accept no less.

Finally, let us look at the contents of the ark: a golden jar holding the manna, Aaron's rod that budded, and the tables of the covenant (see Heb. 9:4). It is not until this New Testament account that we learn that the jar containing the memorial manna was made of gold. God had given instruction that an omerful of the manna was to be placed before the testimony to be kept (see Ex. 16:33–34), but there is no mention of gold.

Israel had grumbled and yearned for the food they enjoyed as slaves in Egypt. Despite their complaints, God provided quail in the evening and manna each morning for six of the seven days each week. For forty years, this was the standard diet of this nation. They grumbled—God supplied. What worthiness was there to be seen? Out of pure grace—unmerited favor—God had met their need and sustained them as they wandered in the desert. It is fitting that a golden jar of manna should be "placed . . . before the Testimony, to be kept" (Ex. 16:34). That very God shown to us in the ark is the same God who, centuries later, showed "the surpassing riches of His grace in kindness toward us in Christ Jesus" (Eph. 2:7).

Our Lord Jesus, in talking to the people, corrected their understanding of the manna. They said that Moses gave them the bread out of heaven. Jesus corrected them to say first of all, "It is My Father who gives you the true bread out of heaven" (John 6:32). The listeners responded, "Lord, evermore give us this bread."

He replied, "I am the bread of life; he who comes to Me shall not hunger, and he who believes in Me shall never thirst" (John 6:35). As Israel was fed daily from the hand of God, so must today's child of God find his daily strength from the food that comes from above. Jesus's words, "I am the bread of life," must turn us away from man's supply to find our daily nurture in the Word of God. Leland Wang was a Chinese evangelist who was much used of God to the Chinese people. Every morning he sought his Lord in Bible reading and prayer. So firm was his commitment to this routine that his rule of life became, "No Bible! No breakfast!" Is your every day marked by a beginning with God in the morning? A wise saint said, "Hem the day in the morning with God lest it ravel by evening." The ark, which typifies our Lord Jesus, contained in its midst "a golden jar holding the manna" for our feeding. God's supply is daily strength for daily needs. We cannot walk today on yesterday's feeding.

> Day by day the manna fell
>   Oh, to learn that lesson well
> Still by constant mercy fed
>   Give us, Lord, our daily bread.
>
> "Day by day" the promise reads
>   Daily strength for daily needs
> Cast foreboding fear away
>   Take the manna of today.
>
> Josiah Conder

The second item listed as in the ark was Aaron's rod which budded (see Heb. 9:4). It was following the insurrection of Korah, Dathan and Abiram in Numbers 16 that God took steps to end the contest for the right of priesthood within Israel. Moses was to take a rod from the leader of each tribe and to write that tribe's name on each leader's rod. A rod from Aaron represented the tribe of Levi. These twelve rods, properly identified, were placed in the Tabernacle before the ark. The contest was to be settled by God, who said, "And it will come about that the rod of the man whom I choose will sprout. Thus I shall lessen from upon Myself the grumblings of the sons of Israel, who are grumbling against you" (Num. 17:5). It is interesting that God said to Moses that the grumbling was upon Himself and only incidentally upon Moses. (Bear this in mind the next time the Holy Spirit speaks through your pastor to rebuke some complaint you may have.) The result was dramatic and positive. On the next day, "Behold, the rod of Aaron for the house of Levi had sprouted and put forth buds and produced blossoms, and it bore ripe almonds" (Num. 17:8). It was following this incident that Moses was instructed to "put back the rod of Aaron before the testimony to be kept" (Num. 17:10).

"It bore ripe almonds." It matters not from what tree the other eleven rods came; Aaron's rod was from an almond tree—the awakening tree—the first tree to blossom in the early spring with a shower of snowy white flowers. Aaron's rod had not merely "sprouted," which was to be the proof of the test; "it bore ripe almonds." This symbol of resurrection certified Aaron's priesthood for all time. So it was with our Lord Jesus. God raised Him from the dead (see Luke 24:6; Acts 2:24). He is thereby established as possessor of an everlasting priesthood after the higher order of Melchizedek, "since He always lives to make intercession for them" (Heb. 7:25).

Paul, in his letter to his son in the faith, Timothy, writes, "Remember Jesus Christ, risen from the dead" (2 Tim. 2:8). This exhortation was to make firm the resolve of the young disciple as he met with opposition and as he took up Paul's tasks after the apostle's departure. Likewise, each morning the believer should strengthen his venture into the day with these words: "Remember Jesus Christ, risen!"

The early Christians greeted one another with the words, "The Lord is risen!" The response was, "He is risen indeed!" Some of those believers exchanged this greeting on the day they were facing wild beasts and the flame for their faith; it was that fact, "He is risen indeed!" that prepared them for the ordeal. Modern life in the western world spares us the spectacle of the arena, but many things come into our lives daily which test our faith. We may find ourselves without employment; we or a member of our family may become seriously ill; a loved one may go to be with the Lord and grief overwhelms us. But, remember, "He is risen indeed!" Job's words ring out clearly to us, "And as for me, I know that my Redeemer lives" (Job 19:25). This assurance strengthens and encourages us in these times of sorrow and difficulty.

> I serve a risen Saviour
>   He's in the world today;
> I know that He is living,
>   Whatever men may say;
> I see His hand of mercy,
>   I hear His voice of cheer,
> And just the time I need Him,
>   He's always near.
>
> He lives, He lives, Christ Jesus lives today!
>   He walks with me and talks with me
> Along life's narrow way.
>   He lives, He lives, salvation to impart!
> You ask me how I know He lives:
>   He lives within my heart.
>
>   Alfred H. Ackley

The third item in the ark was "the tables of the covenant" or the law (see Heb. 9:4), which had been placed in the ark according to the specific instructions of God to Moses (see Ex. 25:16,21; 40:20). These tables were the second set of two panels, which God had inscribed with His own hand. Recognizing the inability of the people to keep the Law of Commandments, God included in the Law the substitutionary sacrifices which would enable the penitent to draw near. He was to bring an innocent animal, confess his sin with his hands on the head of the animal and see its life flow out in his stead, and its body be consumed by the fire of the bronze altar. Sin brought death, his own or that of the animal.

What was the nature of the Law that brought about death for the infraction of its requirements? James calls the law "the perfect law, the law of liberty" (James 1:25). Paul points out, "So then, the law is holy, and the commandment is holy and righteous and good" (Rom. 7:12). He also states that "the Law came in that the transgression might increase" (Rom. 5:20). It is God's measuring rod of the law that makes us realize our sin and our guilt. James warns us, "For whoever keeps the whole law and yet stumbles in one point, he has become guilty of all" (James 2:10).

When we read these words we could easily despair. How then shall we be saved? But these grim words arise from the Tables of the Law which were stored in the ark that shows us Christ: "And He who sent Me is with Me; He has not left Me alone, for I always do the things that are pleasing to Him" (John 8:29); "[Christ] . . . committed no sin, nor was any deceit found in His mouth" (1 Pet. 2:22); "I delight to do Thy will, O my God; thy law is within my heart" (Ps. 40:8). These words describe our Lord: "Always . . . pleasing", "committed no sin", "Thy law . . . within my heart." The One—the only One—who could claim and perform the keeping of the law of God was the spotless Lamb of God. Truly this is a fitting climax for the portrait of the Holy One whose likeness we find in the ark. And we find hope in the fact that this perfect One covers our sins.

The structure shows us Christ in all His deity—God with us—the Holy One in the Holiest. The golden pot gives us God's food for God's people; the budding rod sets forth a risen Savior who could not be held in the bonds of death but who rose for our justification; the Tables of the Law present the only One who kept the Law and as the spotless Lamb bore our sins on the cross.

CHAPTER THIRTEEN

THE MERCY SEAT

EXODUS 25:17–22

" And you shall make a mercy seat of pure gold" (Ex. 25:17). One can well imagine the wonder with which Bezalel and Oholiab heard these instructions that Moses had brought back from the mount. "Two cherubim of gold, make them of hammered work at the two ends of the mercy seat" (v. 18). Beaten work again! But how large, how high? We see that the base is to fit inside the molding on the ark, but how high shall we make the cherubim?

With these questions, the two master craftsmen and their associates set to work leaving the unanswered questions for solving as the work progressed. Thousands of hammer blows rained on the slab of gold. It slowly took form so that a cherub arose from each end of the slab. The base was fitted into the Ark and the wings of the cherubim gracefully pointed upward to form a canopy over the base. The face of each cherub was turned downward as though in ready awe to behold the ceremony appointed for the mercy seat.

"And there I will meet with you, and from above the mercy seat, from between the two cherubim which are upon the ark of the testimony, I will speak to you about all that I will give you in commandment for the sons of Israel" (Ex. 25:22). When the Tabernacle was set up and placed in use, God's presence first appeared between the cherubim (see Ex. 40:34–35). The cloud settled over the Tabernacle, and from that day forward the cloud over the Tabernacle, and later the Temple, signified the presence of Jehovah in communion with His people.

"Of pure gold!" Only one other piece of furniture, the lampstand, carried this specification. The absence of wood gives us an exhibition of pure deity. This top for the ark was representative of our Lord Jesus in all His majestic deity. Here the true God asserted His glory, which He would not share with any other. "I am the Lord, that is My name; I will not give My glory to another, nor My praise to graven images" (Is. 42:8). In a later passage Isaiah uses the same term with an interesting difference. "For My own sake, for My own sake, I will act; for how can My name be profaned? And My glory I will not give to another" (Isa. 48:11). Here God is saying that there is a task to be performed, and He has determined that He must take this work upon Himself. This He did at Calvary.

> There was no other good enough
>   To pay the price of sin;
> He only could unlock the gate
>   Of heaven and let us in.
>
> Cecil F. Alexander

The mercy seat is another type on which the Word of God speaks clearly concerning its meaning. In the third century B.C., a translation of the Hebrew Scriptures into Greek was begun reportedly on the orders of the Egyptian Pharaoh who wanted this volume for his library at Alexandria. It is known as the Septuagint ("seventy") because of the number of scholars said to be involved in the project—seventy-two. In translating the word rendered "mercy seat" in Exodus 25:17, the Greek word "hylasterion" ("propitiation") was used. This same word was used by Paul in his Epistle to the Romans—"Being justified as a gift by His grace through the redemption which is in Christ Jesus; whom God displayed publicly as a propitiation in His blood through faith" (Rom. 3:24–25). The English word, "propitiation", might be rendered more clearly, "a propitiatory." An alternate wording of the verse in Romans could thus be, "Christ Jesus, whom God displayed publicly as a mercy seat." This same Greek word is translated "mercy seat" in Hebrews 9:5. A variation of the word is translated "propitiation" in 1 John 2:2 and 4:10. Thus, we see that the Old Testament word for this very special piece of furniture in the Most Holy Place is used to describe the place where the work of our Lord Jesus was attested to before God. This idea fits well with that of the bronze altar, which, as you will recall from chapter 3, was a very clear type of the cross. There the innocent sacrificial animal represented our Lord Jesus as the Lamb of God giving Himself as the substitute for the believing sinner.

The word "to propitiate" speaks of an act which will placate, appease, or make full satisfaction to the offended party. In this case, it is God whose holy Law has been violated. The penalty for these transgressions against the Law must be fully paid. Our Lord Jesus has taken our place, suffered our penalty, and made propitiation to God for us.

In order to understand fully the function and the meaning of the mercy seat, let us give attention to the ceremony of the Day of Atonement. I pointed out in an earlier chapter the *one* tribe, that of Levi, that lived in the area immediately surrounding the Tabernacle, the *one* family,

Aaron's, that served in the worship at the Tabernacle and the *one* man, the high priest (the first was Aaron), who alone could venture beyond the veil, and then only once a year.

In Leviticus 16, God gave Moses specific instructions for Aaron's approach to Him. The high priest "shall not enter at any time into the holy place inside the veil, before the mercy seat which is on the ark, lest he die; for I will appear in the cloud over the mercy seat" (Lev. 16:2). The word "any" did not preclude the one entry on the Day of Atonement but was intended to exclude entry at any other time as is clarified by the verses which follow in Leviticus 16.

Aaron was to bring, for himself and his family, a bull for a sin offering and a ram for a burnt offering. In addition, he was to take two male goats for the congregation. Then he was to lay aside his robes of office and, after bathing his body, put on special undergarments, a holy tunic, sash, and turban—all of linen.

The bull was to be slaughtered as a sin offering for himself and his family. From this offering, he was to take a bowl of the blood, along with a firepan full of coals from the bronze altar and two handfuls of finely ground sweet incense. No other priest was to be with him in the Holy Place at this time. Then came the climactic moment when he drew aside the veil and stepped in the Holy of Holies. He moved with deliberate haste to cast the incense on the coals of the firepan that the smoke from the incense might fill the room and obscure, if only for a moment, the ark and the mercy seat. With holy anticipation, he dipped his finger in the blood and sprinkled a drop on the east side of the mercy seat. He then returned to the bowl seven times, each time to sprinkle blood on the ground before the ark. With this done, he likely hurried out of the Holiest place to complete the ceremony.

The two goats were for the congregation, and one was chosen by lot for the Lord and was offered as the sin offering. Again, blood of the sacrifice was caught in a bowl. The live goat was chosen as the scapegoat. With Aaron's hands upon its head, the sins of the people were confessed. The scapegoat was led away into the wilderness never to be seen again. Meanwhile, Aaron again entered the Holiest with the blood of the goat. The sprinkling, once on the mercy seat and seven times before the ark, was repeated. Then, returning quickly to the Holy Place, atonement was made by the sprinkling of blood on the golden altar, the table, and the lampstand. On the outside in the courtyard, he smeared blood on the four horns of the bronze altar and sprinkled blood seven times before it. Any defilement of the tent of meeting would be atoned for by this ceremony.

Aaron returned to the Tabernacle, once more bathed his body, put off the linen garments, resumed his robes of office, and came forth to offer the ram as his burnt offering. The return of the high priest to his people signified that all had gone well and that the atonement had been accepted.

The text in Leviticus 16:30 sums up the day of sacrifice this way: "It is on this day that atonement shall be made for you to cleanse you; you shall be clean from all your sins before the Lord."

The bringing of the blood into the Holiest was evidence that the animal sacrifices required by Jehovah had been made. The blood of propitiation, which had been shed at the Bronze Altar, had been sprinkled on the propitiatory or mercy seat as proof that God's requirements had been fully met.[1]

When we read that Christ was set forth by God as the propitiatory, we are brought back to the Day of Atonement ceremony. Christ is the Lamb of God who has shed

His blood by taking our place and suffering our penalty on the cross.

But, note carefully, the words in Romans 3 state that Christ is a propitiatory in His blood through faith. But why blood? As we turn the pages of God's book, we find the divine requirement that blood be shed as the atonement for sin. This requirement goes back beyond Tabernacle days. In the earliest history of the human race, we find God shedding the blood of innocent animals that He might make the coats of skins to cover the nakedness of the sinning couple, Adam and Eve. The shedding of blood is repeated in Abel's offering. The writer to the Hebrews tells us that "By faith Abel offered to God a better sacrifice than Cain, through which he obtained the testimony that he was righteous" (Heb. 11:4). The act of faith speaks of obedience, and obedience speaks of a commandment which directed his offering. Thus we conclude that God had communicated to Abel His divine will in this matter. Abraham, too, learned about the shedding of blood as God's command for atonement. He also saw God's mercy, for as he raised the knife to slay his only son, God stopped him in mid-stroke and substituted the ram which He Himself had provided.

The Hebrews had been slaves of Pharaoh in Egypt. A great contest was raging between God, through His messenger Moses, and Pharaoh. One by one the gods of the Egyptians—the Nile, the scarab, the Sun, the cattle—had been judged by God. The Pharaoh, himself, was considered a god; he was the next to be judged. After Pharaoh reneged on his promises, he was brought face to face with the ultimate contest. The word came that God would go out into the midst of Egypt, "and all the first-born in the land of Egypt shall die, from the first-born of the Pharaoh who sits on his throne, even to the first-born of the slave girl who is behind the millstones; all the first-born of the cattle as well" (Ex. 11:5). Then follow the instructions to the Israelites as to their action to protect their households from the death angel. They were to take a lamb for each household. If the household was too small to eat an entire lamb they were to join with a neighbor in the activity so that "according to what each man should eat, you are to divide the lamb" (Ex. 12:4). In Exodus 12:5, the sacrifice to be used had a personal title; it is described as "your lamb." It was to be without blemish, a male a year old.

The lamb was to be slain and some of its blood was to be sprinkled on the two doorposts and the lintel of each Hebrew house. When the death angel saw this blood, he was to pass over that household. "No plague will befall you to destroy you when I strike the land of Egypt" (Ex. 12:13).

With these instructions, Israel set about making preparations for the fateful night. One can well imagine the lambs that had taken on the status of pets during the preparatory period and the appeals of children to keep the animal in the house. The house that yielded to such entreaties placed itself in peril. It was the blood of the lamb *slain* that gave protection, and the house that ignored the warning must be prepared to pay the price. "When I see the blood" was the unqualified instruction, and the blow fell as God had said it would. Where there was blood—no death. Where there was no blood—death.

In Exodus 12:30 we read that "there was no home where there was not someone dead." In Pharaoh's palace, the first-born lay dead; in the home of the slave girl behind the millstones, the first-born lay dead; and yes, in the houses of Israel with the blood on the doorposts and lintel, even there was death. It was the lamb, whose shed blood provided the protection on that night of terror.

The whole tenor of the Levitical offering called for the shedding of the blood of an innocent substitute for the penitent sinner. In Leviticus 17:11 we read, "For the life of the flesh is in the blood, and I have given it to you on the altar to make atonement for your souls; for it is the blood by reason of the life that makes atonement." That Jehovah should call for the shedding of blood would not seem strange to Israel. The Passover night was still vivid in their memory. When God said to them, "It is the blood . . . that makes atonement," their thoughts would return to the night of their deliverance.

The account in Hebrews 9 tells of the inauguration of the first covenant with blood. When the Tabernacle was completed and set up, Moses "took the blood of the calves and the goats, with water and scarlet wool and hyssop, and sprinkled both the book itself and all the people, saying, 'This is the blood of the covenant which God commanded you.' And in the same way he sprinkled both the tabernacle and all the vessels of the ministry with the blood" (Heb. 9:19–21).

The New Testament abounds with references to the necessity of blood for forgiveness of sins. When our Lord gave the cup to His disciples, He looked forward to the cross and said, "This cup . . . is the new covenant in My blood" (Luke 22:20). Paul writes to the Ephesians, "You who formerly were far off have been brought near by the blood of Christ" (Eph. 2:13). Peter reminds us that we have not been "redeemed with perishable things like silver or gold . . . but with precious blood . . . of Christ" (1 Peter 1:18–19). John's word to his beloved Christians is that "the blood of Jesus . . . cleanses us from all sin" (1 John 1:7). The writer to the Hebrews states, "without shedding of blood there is no forgiveness" (Heb. 9:22).

For us today, as for the patriarchs and then Israel in

Egypt, the providing of the blood for atonement and forgiveness requires our positive step of faith in claiming the atoning blood of Jesus as our own.

There is a story told of a man, a tight-wire walker, who had stretched a wire across the chasm at Niagara Falls. With great fanfare, he advertised that he would walk the wire. On the day of the event a large crowd assembled to watch the spectacle. He walked part of the way across and back. The applause was loud and long. He began to taunt the crowd. Singling out one enthusiastic man on the front row, he said to him. "Do you believe I can walk all the way across the wire"?

"Yes" was the enthusiastic answer.

"You have no doubt?"

"No—none."

"Do you think I can walk across the wire carrying a man on my back?"

The answer was almost as quick, "Yes, I do."

"Will you be that man?" With that question the enthusiast drew back and disappeared into the crowd.

We may read about the blood, but until we really put our personal trust in what Christ has done, it is of no avail. "Will you be that man?"

Our Lord Jesus, our Great High Priest, has "entered through the greater and more perfect tabernacle, not made with hands, that is to say, not of this creation; and not through the blood of goats and calves, but through His own blood, He entered the holy place once for all, having obtained eternal redemption" (Heb. 9:11–12). We see here clearly the fulfilling of the mercy seat type. I believe that the text here is more than dramatic prose and that our Lord actually performed the ceremonies described. This possibility is indicated by His words to Mary after His resurrection, "I have not yet ascended to the Father . . . I ascend to My Father and your Father, and My God and your God" (John 20:17). Thus the type of the propitiation has had its completion. We can now rejoice in the words which follow our previous reference in Hebrews: "For if the blood of goats and bulls and the ashes of a heifer sprinkling those who have been defiled, sanctify for the cleansing of the flesh, how much more will the blood of Christ, who through the eternal Spirit offered Himself without blemish to God, cleanse your conscience from dead works to serve the living God?" (Heb. 9:13–14). We now look upon the mercy seat and find there the blood of our Savior and know that we have been justified (Rom. 5:9).

> There is a place where Jesus sheds
>   The oil of gladness on our heads,
> A place than all besides more sweet
>   It is the blood-bought mercy seat.

>   Hugh Stowell

Romans 3:25 contains two tremendous words— "displayed publicly"—that put statements of the verse in a special light. Neither we nor the world can escape the events of Calvary. The crucifixion and resurrection of our Lord resounded throughout the Roman Empire so that Caesar himself took knowledge of the events. Historians, scientists, statesmen and generals alike have marked off this thirty-two year period as the turning point in their calculations—B.C.—before Christ; A.D., "anno domini" (the year of our Lord) or C.E.—the Christian Era. God saw to it that His "public display" of grace and mercy would be burned into the consciousness of all peoples.

The return of the high priest to the congregation is a part of the ceremony rich in teaching that we must not overlook. As we shall see in our next chapter, the high priest's robe had around its hem a decoration of golden bells and pomegranates, alternately one after the other. The account tells us that the purpose of the bells was that "its tinkling may be heard when he enters and leaves the holy place before the Lord, that he may not die" (Ex. 28:35). The congregation of Israel was waiting expectantly as the high priest went into the tent of meeting to perform the ceremony with blood and incense. It was clear what was required and what might be expected, but there was an understandable anxiety that all would go well. During the ceremonies of the Day of Atonement the people were gathered in the area surrounding the Tabernacle court. After the high priest's disappearance, they waited for his return, which would signify that all was well, and that the sprinkling of the blood had been accepted. Those in the front rows might be able to see, but those farther back depended on someone's relaying to them words as to the progress of events. The first signal of the high priest's accomplishment of the mission and his return to the people was the tinkling of the bells on his garment. All was well and word was passed through the ranks, "We have heard the bells!"

Our Lord Jesus has passed into Heaven with His own blood and our redemption is sure. One day He will rise from His throne and come forth to claim His bride, along with the believers of all ages. As the clock of history ticks on, we look upon the events with happy anticipation. It seems we hear the tinkling of the bells announcing His coming. Soon we shall hear the trumpet, the shout, and the wonderful words, "Arise, my darling, my beautiful one, and come along" (Song 2:10); and we shall rise to meet Him.

A fragment of a hymn rings in my memory—

Thou art coming, O my Saviour,
    Thou art coming, O my King!
In Thy beauty all resplendent;
    In Thy glory all transcendent;
Well may we rejoice and sing:
    Coming! in the opening east
Herald brightness slowly swells;
    Coming! O my glorious Priest,
Hear we not Thy golden bells?

Frances R. Havergal

To be ready for the day of His appearing, we need first to place our personal trust in Christ as our Savior. The way into the Holiest has been made open. There is no longer a bar to our access. The blood of Christ has been carried into the heavenly Tabernacle, and we may draw near with confidence since we know that "Christ also, having been offered once to bear the sins of many, shall appear a second time, . . . to those who eagerly await Him" (Heb. 9:28).

CHAPTER FOURTEEN

THE HIGH PRIEST'S GARMENTS

EXODUS 28:1–43; 39:1–32

"Holy garments . . . for glory and for beauty!" (Ex. 28:2). These words describe the wardrobe that was an essential part of the worship carried on in Jehovah's Tabernacle. To omit these wonderful items from our study would be like passing over the cornerstone in the structure of a building. There is no doubt that the buildings, furniture, vessels, ministration, and garments all refer to one subject. God writes His own comment immediately following the instructions on the garments. "Thus all the work of the tabernacle of the tent of meeting was completed; and the sons of Israel did according to all that the Lord had commanded Moses; so they did" (Ex. 39:32).

The Tabernacle and its vessels were useless without the priesthood. We have observed that Aaron and his sons were divinely chosen that they might minister before God. There is grace in this selection. Aaron, Moses's brother, had weakly consented to the people in their rebellion, building the golden calf and participating in their revels while Moses was on the mountain with God (see Ex. 32:1–5). Yet this was the man whom God chose to lead the worship in the Tabernacle. When we, who are at best unprofitable servants, are used of God in making Christ known, we can understand His choice of Aaron to lead His people in worship.

In our study of the ark, we read that "Aaron's rod that budded" was laid up in the ark for a perpetual testimony that Aaron and his sons had been chosen by God as priests before Him. Moses was to take "Aaron your brother, and his sons with him . . . to minister as priest to Me" (Ex. 28:1). Successors to Aaron must come from his family and become priests by virtue of their relationship to their father. They were to exercise the offering of sacrifices and to conduct the worship of the Holy Place. Theirs was the responsibility for teaching statutes. One alone, who succeeded to the high priest's office, could carry out the ceremonies on the Day of Atonement. All priests received their assignments and duties from the high priest who was the unquestioned authority during his term in office. They acted on behalf of all the people in the offering of sacrifices and in intercession.

We read in Hebrews 5:1, "Every high priest taken from among men is appointed on behalf of men in things pertaining to God." He is also called upon to "deal gently with" or better, to love "the ignorant and misguided" (v. 2). Thus, in Old Testament times, he had a major task in maintaining fellowship between the believer and God. He could not secure God's favor with the people, but he could and did take an active role in maintaining fellowship with God. If the child of God today has fallen into grievous sin, it is the privilege of a fellow believer-priest to love that one and gently point him back to the Savior's fellowship. The pastor (or layman) who functions effectively in this field is certainly demonstrating the grace of God in action. Our Lord Jesus encouraged Peter to "tend My lambs," "tend My sheep," (John 21:15,17). Tending takes time,

The High Priest's Garments

patience, and love, and this includes dealing gently. We may wonder how often Peter said to himself, as he ministered in Christ's name,—"This comes under the heading of tending lambs." Has God given you some of His lambs to tend?

It is interesting to note that God gave instructions for the garments before He gave instructions for the ordination. However, before considering the garments in detail, let us look into the consecration of Aaron, which is of interest at this point. We should be well aware that many of the events of Aaron's consecration, as well as the description of his garments, point to the establishing of believers as priests unto God (see 1 Pet. 2:9).

The ceremony of consecration lasted for seven days. Moses was to take one young bull and two rams without blemish, unleavened bread, unleavened cakes mixed with oil, and unleavened wafers spread with oil. The bread, cakes, and wafers were put in a basket and presented along with the bull and the two rams.

Aaron and his sons were brought to the doorway of the tent of meeting and washed with water. This washing points forward to the new birth, where Jesus Himself spoke of the necessity of one's being "born of water and the Spirit" (John 3:5). This washing was not repeated. Likewise we, being born again by receiving Christ as Savior, have no need to repeat this step. We are born again, once and for all.

Aaron was then garbed in the seven pieces of his robes, starting with linen breeches, a linen tunic and a sash or girdle. Then followed the robe or coat of the ephod, all in blue, woven in one piece and providing holes for the arms and head. The robe reached almost to the ground and had around its hem a decoration of pomegranates of blue, purple, and scarlet alternating with bells of pure gold. The bells tinkled as the high priest moved in his ministering.

The next was a very beautiful garment, the ephod. This consisted of two panels, each reaching from shoulder to shoulder and falling in front and back to the loins. At each shoulder a strap joined the two panels forming a sort of vest. Each strap was highlighted by an onyx stone set in gold filigree, bearing the names of the sons of Israel engraved across its face.

The most magnificent and valuable item was the breastpiece. On its face were twelve precious stones set in gold— one for each of the tribes. The breastpiece was folded double to form a pouch in which the high priest carried the Urim and Thummim. The magnificent ephod and its breastpiece was also finished off by a sash or girdle of the ephod. This served to bind the ephod to the high priest's body and relieve some of the weight.

The head was covered by a turban of pure white linen wrapped much in the manner of Indians of New Delhi or Agra. A plate of pure gold bearing the engraving, "Holy to the Lord", was bound to the front of the turban by gold chains.

After Aaron was robed, Moses took the vessel of anointing oil and poured it on Aaron's head.

Following the dressing of the high priest was the presentation of a young bull and two rams without blemish, along with unleavened bread, cakes, and wafers with varying portions of oil. Aaron and his sons placed their hands on the head of the bull, after which it was slaughtered and some of the blood smeared on the four horns of the bronze altar. The remainder of the blood was poured out at the base of the altar. Portions of the bull were then offered up in smoke on the altar. The flesh of the bull, its hide and refuse, were burned outside the camp. Aaron and his sons laid their hands on the head of the first ram, which was then slaughtered and offered as a whole burnt offering. A third time Aaron and his sons laid their hands on the head of an animal (the second ram), which was also slaughtered. Moses took some of the blood of this animal and put it on the lobe of the right ear of Aaron and his sons, on the thumbs of their right hands and the great toes of their right feet. More blood was sprinkled around the altar. Oil was then applied over the blood on their right ears, thumbs, and great toes. This part of the ceremony makes clear that the Holy Spirit, as symbolized by the oil, comes only after the blood of redemption has been applied. Blood from the altar and some of the anointing oil were sprinkled on both Aaron and his garments, completing the consecration.

In Hebrews 3:1 we are instructed to "consider Jesus, the Apostle and High Priest of our confession." Let us, therefore, examine more closely the garments of Aaron, where we shall find a beautiful, spiritual portrait of our risen Lord Jesus, our Great High Priest.

The inner garments of breeches, tunic, and sash were of pure white byssus linen. These garments of white symbolized the righteous way of life required of the priests. Psalm 132:9 reads, "Let Thy priests be clothed with righteousness." The priest who was to serve in the Tabernacle was required to be physically perfect. Any defect in his physical makeup would disqualify him. The ceremony of consecration made him ceremonially pure and holy. This quality of holiness was to mark him as long as he lived. There were precise restrictions as to whom he could marry. His wife was to be a virgin of his own people, neither a widow, a divorced woman, one polluted, nor a harlot (see Lev. 21:13–15). He was to have no contact with death, even for his father or mother (see Lev. 21:10–11). He was not to rend his clothes or defile himself in any way. This was the man who was divinely appointed to represent the congregation before the Lord as mediator. It was not an office sought after or gained by popular election. He received divine communications and transmitted them to the people. He was the representative of the ever-living God.

Our Lord Jesus was subject to intense scrutiny by all manner of inquisitors during His years on this earth. Before all of them, He did not sin. No one could point to that which would mar His spotless humanity. Beginning with His baptism, the Holy Spirit proclaimed His holy person (see John 1:32). Demons acknowledged Him (see Mark 1:23–24). Pilate and Herod found no fault in Him (see Matt. 27:24; Luke 23:13–15). Stephen's testimony was that He was "the Righteous One" (see Acts 7:52). Peter, John, Paul, and the writer to the Hebrews join in stating that He was without sin. Seven times in the New Testament Jesus is described as "righteous" or "just." On the Mount of Transfiguration, God the Father spoke the final word when He stated, "This is My beloved Son, with whom I am well-pleased; hear Him!" (Matt. 17:5).

The undergarments of the High Priest were completed with a sash, translated in the King James Version as "girdle." The purpose of the sash or girdle was to fasten the loose Eastern garments more securely about the body so as not to impede movement. The high priest was active in his work, and this sash served to give him freedom as he moved to and fro. In John 13:4 Jesus, in a dramatic gesture, "rose from supper, and laid aside His garments; and taking a towel, girded Himself about." There follows that moving scene of Jesus washing the disciples' feet, even Judas's. This picture of humble service leaves with us the portrait of Christ who came to serve (see Luke 22:27). He emptied Himself and took the form of a bondservant and was obedient to the point of death on the cross (see Phil. 2:7–8). The garments for service became our Lord Jesus, for it was through His service that we have been redeemed and seated in heavenly places with Him (see Eph. 1:3).

Peter encourages believers to "gird your minds for action" (1 Pet. 1:13), thereby calling for alertness on the part of the believer-priest. He warns against laxness and calls to the mind of believers all that each has received now and is to receive at the coming of our Lord. We are called to serve one another and to love one another, the hallmarks of the early Christians.

The robe of the ephod was the next piece of clothing for the high priest. It was all of blue and woven in one piece including the openings for the head and arms. As previously mentioned, the blue speaks of our High Priest's heavenly character and the perfection of its manufacture proclaims One who was completely one with His Father and who came from the Father (see John 14:11; 17:8). He is now our Heavenly High Priest who ministers on our behalf. Never forget, child of God, that we are "partakers of a heavenly calling" (see Heb. 3:1). We have a heavenly citizenship (see Phil. 3:20). We are also the possessors of a heavenly inheritance which is being guarded by sentinels, reserved in heaven for us (see 1 Pet. 1:4). He, as the Heavenly One, waits at the right hand of the Father (see 1 Cor. 15:47; Heb. 8:1) where He is preparing a place for us (see John 14:2).

In a previous chapter, we took a brief look at the bells on the hem of this full length robe. Between each bell of pure gold was the semblance of a pomegranate in one of three colors—blue, purple, or scarlet. As the high priest moved, these bells tinkled to indicate his presence. We noted the special significance of the bells on the Day of Atonement and how they should turn our gaze to the sky to look for "the blessed hope and the appearing . . . of our great God and Savior, Christ Jesus" (Titus 2:13). The tinkling of the bells indicated to those who would hear that the high priest was active on behalf of the people. In Hebrews 8:1 we read the assuring statement, "Now the main point in what has been said is this: We have such a high priest." God would underscore this for us. We *have* a high priest, and He is God's own Son in glory.

Over the robe was placed the ephod, which was a beautiful garment. Here for the first time we find gold worked into the fabric along with the usual colors—blue, purple, scarlet, and white linen. It is fitting that in the ephod, gold should make its appearance. It was pure gold, beaten into plates and cut into wires—not some color simulating gold.

While the four usual colors appear to remind us of our Lord's heavenly origin in the blue, His royal descent in the purple, His suffering service in the scarlet, and His spotless humanity in the linen, we are brought face to face with the addition of pure gold. He was and is all that we have seen in past chapters; but the gold wires woven into the patterns would emphasize to us His deity without having it mixed in any way with His humanity. He was very God and He was very man. He slept the sleep of human exhaustion during a storm at sea, yet He stilled the raging waves with a word as their Maker (see Mark 4:39). When Peter told the tax collectors that Jesus paid taxes to a human government, He commanded a fish of His creation to swim onto Peter's hook. The fish would yield a coin of the correct amount with which to pay the tax for both Himself and Peter. An earthly obligation was discharged by an act of omnipotence (see Matt. 17:27). At Lazarus's tomb He wept the tears of human grief, but the words of the Creator bade Lazarus rise (see John 11:43). In none of these and many other cases was there a mixture. Truly, this was the

Word made flesh, the High Priest, the Son of God (see John 1:14; Heb. 4:14).

The two panels of the ephod were joined at the shoulders by two straps of the same material which bore golden settings, containing in each an onyx stone on which the names of the twelve sons of Israel were engraved—six on each stone: on the left, Gad, Asher, Issachar, Zebulun, Joseph, Benjamin; on the right, Reuben, Simeon, Levi, Judah, Dan, Naphtali. Today we tend to look down on onyx stones as being rather low in value. It is believed that these stones were of the sardonyx variety which has streaks of black, white, and red—a beautiful stone which I have seen in the Taj Mahal. Job compared wisdom to the "precious onyx" in value (see Job 28:16).

The names were engraved "according to their birth" (see Ex. 28:10). Herein we find no recognition of achievement nor wealth, but simply according to their birth were they engraved. Each believer has a secure place before God. Our names are engraved—not written—and cannot be erased. It is by the new birth that we stand, and no special achievement is required. We can do nothing to add to or subtract from our standing before God. The humblest believer is named alongside those of noble birth or worldly fame, having the same righteousness, the same justification.

The two onyx stones rested on the high priest's shoulders—a place of strength and security. Wherever he went, the stones went. They were stones "for a memorial" (see Ex. 28:12). The names were never to be forgotten. Similarly, when we rest on God's shoulders, it is His strength that supports us (see Is. 9:6). It is His perseverance that keeps us (see 2 Tim. 1:12). He who "upholds all things by the word of His power" (Heb. 1:3) is willing and able to uphold the humblest saint. The shepherd (with one lost sheep) found it, placed it on his shoulders, carried it all the way home, and then called for his friends to rejoice with him. Fear not, troubled one, your High Priest has your name on His shoulders and will see you all the way home. In John 10:3 we read these precious words, "He calls his own sheep by name."

On the front of the ephod was a special pouch made of linen, beautifully embroidered with gold, blue, purple and scarlet. This is the first piece of clothing mentioned in Exodus 28:4. It was without a doubt the foremost in beauty and most costly of all the wardrobe. When folded double to form the pouch, the breastpiece, as it was called, measured a span (about 8½ inches) in each direction. On its face were twelve precious stones set in gold—once again, one for each of the tribes of Israel. There were four rows of three, each one bearing the engraved name of the tribe it represented.

1st row	Emerald	Topaz	Ruby
Tribe	Zebulun	Issachar	Judah
2nd row	Diamond	Sapphire	Turquoise
Tribe	Gad	Simeon	Reuben
3rd row	Amethyst	Agate	Jacinth
Tribe	Benjamin	Manasseh	Ephraim
4th row	Jasper	Onyx	Beryl
Tribe	Naphtali	Asher	Dan

Each was different and each was a precious jewel.

This arrangement was different from that on the shoulder stones. It represented the relative positions of the tribes in the order of the camp beginning with Judah in the place of honor before the eastern door of the Tabernacle.

Each jewel had its own distinctive beauty, but it was

only as the light struck them that the clarity of their nature and the perfection of their facets brought beauty to the eye of the beholder. Greater light brought greater beauty. We are all jewels in the eyes of our Savior, but it is only as we walk in the light that the beauty of Jesus can be seen in us. Some facets require long and careful cutting and grinding to bring out their true beauty. Our heavenly Jeweler knows us and applies the necessary shaping and polishing to ensure that we fill the place He has designed for us in His light.

Of the twelve stones, no two were alike. They were different in form, character, and beauty. Each had its own value in the eyes of men, but they were all gems in the sight of our God. God is gathering His jewels from many lands, from many tongues but all have received of His grace which He freely bestowed on us in the Beloved (see Eph. 1:6). All have put on or clothed themselves with Christ (see Gal. 3:27), and all have been made complete in Him (see Col. 2:10). There are no second class believers in their standing before God.

The breastpiece was on the front of the ephod and immediately over Aaron's heart. To add to the security of the breastpiece, there were two rings of gold at the bottom edge, which were connected with two other rings of gold on the ephod by cords of blue. In addition, there were two rings of gold at the top of the breastpiece which were connected to the settings for the shoulder stones by cordage work of gold. The name on each stone was engraved on it, "like the engravings of a seal" (Ex. 28:21). In Solomon's Song 8:6, we read these beautiful words: "Put me like a seal over your heart." And so we are—a seal over the heart of our Lord. Thus we have an example of our security made sure by our heavenly and divine Lord who carries us on His heart.

Consider our Lord's ministry for us today. He entered "into heaven itself, now to appear in the presence of God for us" (Heb. 9:24). How comforting is the thought that He is always at the right hand of God interceding for us. He makes His claims on our behalf and presents us with joy as those God has given Him (see John 17:11; Heb. 2:13). We are the ones for whom He died. We are cleansed with His blood and are the objects of His love. There is the eternal connection between His shoulders of strength and His heart of love; He cannot and will not fail us nor forsake us. He has undertaken our cause and will never lay it down. He knows no fatigue nor loss of interest.

Arthur Pink quotes the following about Jesus from the pen of J. N. Darby:

> He preserves us, as that which He has on His heart, to God. He cannot be before Him without doing so, and whatever claim the desires and wishes of Christ's heart has to draw out the favor of God operates in drawing out the favor to us. The light and favor of the sanctuary—God as dwelling there—cannot shine out on Him without shining on us, and that as an object present to Him for it.[1]

Do we consider Jesus in our daily life? I fear that we struggle in this world of sin as though we had no High Priest who has passed into heaven for us, whose every act of loving care is directed to our welfare. Do we limit Him? We cannot outrun His grace or flee from His loving power. Do we seek that place near to the heart of Jesus as we walk every day?

Paul makes three statements of the longings of his heart in Philippians 3: "That I may gain Christ" (3:8), "and may be found in Him" (3:9), "that I may know Him" (3:10). He wanted all that Christ had for him. He sums up these longings with the simple statement, "For to me to live is Christ" (Phil. 1:21). He wanted a place at the center of the heart of Christ, where the divine love and care would envelop him.

Our Lord selected a group of seventy whom He sent out into all of the cities where He Himself planned to go (see Luke 10:1); at another time He chose twelve whom He named apostles (see Luke 6:13) who were to be with Him; there were three, Peter, James, and John, who were His intimates (see Mark 9:2). *But* there was only one who reclined on Jesus's breast; He carried the name of "the disciple whom Jesus loved" (see John 13:23).

Dr. I. M. Haldeman writes:

> It is our privilege to so live down here as Christians that we may continually win the special favor of the Lord and be classified—anyone of us—as "the disciple whom Jesus loved." Saved . . . redeemed . . . made partakers of the divine nature . . . sealed by the indwelling Holy Spirit . . . owned before God . . . made the very righteousness of God in Christ . . . so presented by Him . . . that our standing may not fail. . . . We who believe do not have to live *like* sons of God to become such, but because *we are* sons of God we are to live like sons of God, each day with deeper consciousness of our Lord's measureless love, each day seeking to serve Him more fully until we shall feel the outstretching of His heart to us and know we are closer to its inmost beating every present day than any yesterday.[2]

One further word about our High Priest. The Aaronic high priesthood was in a process of constant change due to death. As each one died, a new one was appointed to take his place. Our Lord is a priest after the order of Melchizedek and ministers in the power of an endless life. He never tires, nor can He forget those whom He has bought at so great a price. "He always lives to make intercession for them" (Heb. 7:25), and ministers in "the power of an indestructible life" (Heb. 7:16).

> Near, so very near to God
>   Nearer I cannot be;
> For in the person of His Son
>   I am as near as He.
>
> So dear, so very dear to God
>   Dearer I cannot be
> The love wherewith He loves the Son
>   Such is His love to me.
>
> Anonymous

Upon Aaron's head was a turban of pure white linen. This distinguished him from the priests of lesser rank who wore caps. In Bible days, the covering of the head signified obedience. Truly, the high priest was the servant of Jehovah.

Christ is seen before us as the obedient One who sought His Father's will, not His own (see Luke 22:42). He became "obedient to the point of death" (Phil. 2:8). Isaiah speaks of Christ as "My Servant" (Is. 42:1). How this stands in contrast with our day when self is enthroned and self-esteem is sought after. God is seeking those who will dethrone self and accept His rule in their life.

On the front of the turban was fastened, with cords of blue, a plate of pure gold on which were engraved the words, "Holy to the Lord" (Ex. 28:36). This was to be fastened to Aaron's forehead in order that he might make acceptable the gifts the people brought for service (see Ex. 28:38). He was devoted in his representation of the people before God, and the holiness of life required of him was seen in the meaning of the plate. In whatever portion of the service he participated, be it great or small, he carried the words, "Holy to the Lord." There was nothing that did not bear this stamp.

As believer-priests, we have the opportunity of first presenting our bodies as "a living and holy sacrifice, acceptable to God" (Rom. 12:1). From there we go on to render the "sacrifice of praise to God" (Heb. 13:15); the service of witnessing to the saving power of Christ; the cup of cold water in His name; the kindly word or the tender touch. These also are to be "Holy to the Lord."

Holiness of life is God's ultimate expectation for each of His children. There is no option here, for 1 Thessalonians 4:3 tells us that "This is the will of God, your sanctification." There can be no rest in outward forms and no trust in rites.

Inside the pouch of the breastpiece were two gems identified in the text as the Urim and Thummim. The literal translation of the two Hebrew words gives them names, "lights and perfections." The Greek words in the Septuagint Old Testament are "manifestations and truth." These mysterious articles are referred to seven times in the Old Testament; four times as the Urim and the Thummim (Ex. 28:30; Lev. 8:8; Ezra 2:63; Neh. 7:65); once in Deut. 33:8 as the Thummim and Urim; and twice in Num. 27:21 and 1 Sam. 28:6 as the Urim alone.

There is no record of their making, but it is known that they were carried in the pouch of the breastpiece and that the will of God was conveyed through them. A question or decision required was stated, and one stone was drawn from the pouch, indicating God's decision. It was a form of lots, and there are many references to the lot falling out in a certain way (see Joshua 17:4–5; 18:11; 19:17). Joshua, with Eleazar, the priest who had the Urim and Thummim, where charged with the dividing of the land (see Num.

34:17). Earlier Moses had been commanded to commission Joshua as his successor with the reassuring word that, "He shall stand before Eleazar, the priest, who shall inquire for him by the judgment of the Urim before the Lord" (Num. 27:21). David inquired of the Lord before entering into battle with the Philistines (see 1 Sam. 23:2). Later in Israel's history, there was a question as to the genealogies of some of the sons of priests returning from the captivity. It was ruled that these men should not eat from the most holy things until the priest stood up with Urim and Thummim (see Ezra 2:63). From these Scriptures we can conclude that the breastpiece of judgment provided decisions on matters of government, warfare, and worship to Israel.

We again remind ourselves that these two stones, which weighed so heavily in Israel's day-to-day activities, rested in the high priest's pouch, directly over his heart, and thus from a position of deep love and care, gave forth their fateful decisions.

In our Lord, we find many of the characteristics of the Urim and Thummim. In the Urim (lights), we find Him "full of grace and truth" (John 1:14). He was "the true light which, coming into the world, enlightens every man" (John 1:9). He was "the light of the world" (John 8:12). Paul points out that we have "the light of the knowledge of the glory of God in the face of Christ" (2 Cor. 4:6).

Regarding Jesus's likeness to the Thummim (perfections), we read Paul's statement that as for His deity, our Lord is "over all, God blessed forever" (Rom. 9:5). As for His humanity, he was "the holy offspring" (Luke 1:35) who was openly recognized by the Father as "My beloved Son, with whom I am well-pleased; hear Him!" (Matt. 17:5). David, writing prophetically in Psalm 45:2, says, "Grace is poured upon Thy lips; therefore God has blessed

Thee forever." Peter speaks of Him as "a lamb unblemished and spotless" (1 Pet. 1:19). Truly He represented "perfections."

Jesus bears other titles that become Him as the source of wisdom and light for the believer. Isaiah identifies Him as "Wonderful Counselor" (Is. 9:6). Paul writes of Him "in whom are hidden all the treasures of wisdom and knowledge" (Col. 2:3). Jesus, to His disciples, makes the simple yet profound statement, "I am . . . the truth" (John 14:6).

Considering our Lord once again in His office of Great High Priest, we must realize that such a One who bears us on His heart of love and shoulders of strength carries on His heart His will and purpose for us. The mind and will of God were perfectly revealed to Him and by Him. He has done always those "things that are pleasing to [God]" (John 8:29). He has had "all things handed over to" Him by His Father, and it is He who reveals the Father to us (Matt. 11:27). When speaking with His disciples after the Last Supper, the Lord opens His heart to say, "No longer do I call you slaves; for the slave does not know what his master is doing; but I have called you friends, for all things that I have heard of My Father I have made known to you" (John 15:15). To His friends, our Lord Jesus divulges the judgments and decisions of God. The Holy Spirit is the messenger of the Godhead to transmit these instructions for the most minute aspects of our pilgrim life. There is no reason to grope our way through the maze. We have a Savior, our High Priest, who knows the way we should take, and He waits to direct our steps and our stops when we pause long enough to let Him speak to us. His decisions come from His heart, and we need have no fear to follow.

"Consider Jesus, the Apostle and High Priest of our confession" (Heb. 3:1). We *have* such a High Priest.

CHAPTER FIFTEEN

THE OFFERINGS

LEVITICUS 1:1—7:38

We will now look in detail at the sacrifices or offerings to which I have repeatedly referred in passing. When the Tabernacle was completed, God spoke to Moses from the Tent of Meeting, giving His instructions for the offerings (Lev. 1:1).

Alfred Edersheim gives the following introductory comment on the offerings:

> The sacrifices of the Old Testament were symbolical and typical. An outward observance without any real inward meaning is only a ceremony. But a rite which has a present spiritual meaning is a symbol; and if, besides, it also points to a future reality, conveying at the same time, by anticipation the blessing that is yet to appear, it is a type. Thus, the Old Testament sacrifices were not only symbols nor yet merely predictions by fact (as a prophecy is a prediction by word), but they already conveyed to the believing Israelites the blessing that was to flow from the future reality to which they pointed.[1]

All of the offerings, as we shall see, pointed forward in time to the sacrificial death of our Lord Jesus Christ. No one sacrifice, of itself, provides a complete picture of Christ. When they are considered together, they give us a full understanding of what Christ accomplished on the cross. In every offering, there was the element of substitution. The offerer brought the animal and, by placing his hands on its head, identified himself with it; in essence, the two became one.

We shall look at the five offerings: the burnt offering, the grain offering, the peace offering, the sin offering, and the trespass offering. The first three typified God's acceptance of the sinner in his worship; while the last two restored communion with God which had been broken by sin.

The Burnt Offering—Leviticus 1:1–17; 6:9–13

In the burnt offering, we have a type of Christ offering Himself without spot to God. This offering was to be made from the herd, or flock, or of birds, according to the prosperity of the offerer. If it were from the herd, it was to be a bull without defect and was to be offered before the doorway of the Tent of Meeting. The New American Standard Bible reads that a person offered the bull "that he may be accepted before the Lord" (Lev. 1:3). The King James Version renders these words "of his own voluntary will". In both, the idea of a voluntary offering is apparent. Our Lord Jesus was a voluntary offering to God, and His primary objective was to glorify God and do His will. We read in Psalm 40:8, "I delight to do Thy will, O my God; Thy law is within my heart." In John 10:17–18 Jesus states, "I lay down My life that I may take it again. No one has taken it away from Me, but I lay it down on My own initiative. I have authority to lay it down, and I have authority to take it up again."

When crucifixion was before Jesus, "He resolutely set

his face to go to Jerusalem" (Luke 9:51). As He prayed in the garden and the awfulness of being made sin came upon Him, He asked, "If Thou art willing, remove this cup from Me; yet not My will, but Thine be done" (Luke 22:42). He who "existed in the form of God . . . humbled Himself by becoming obedient to the point of death" (Phil. 2:6–8). His whole desire was to do the will of His Father.

Not only was the burnt offering a voluntary offering but the animal had to be without defect. This typified Christ as the offering without defect, which point I have explained before. His human life brought no legitimate criticism or blame. No one was able to accuse Him of sin. Openly He challenged men with, "Which one of you convicts Me of sin?" (John 8:46). The writer to the Hebrews sums up this blameless life with these words, "How much more will the blood of Christ, who through the eternal Spirit offered Himself without blemish to God, cleanse your conscience from dead works to serve the living God?" (Heb. 9:14).

It is true that the sacrifice would be slain and the body consumed on the fire as an atonement, but the question of sinbearing is not before us in the burnt offering. This is reserved for the sin offering.

The sacrificial animal was to be skinned, cut in pieces, and laid in order on the wood. In this, we see the inward life and motives of our Lord made bare. He was without defect in His hidden life and His public life. When Satan tempted Him in the wilderness to exalt Himself, He quoted Scripture in reply.

After the body of the animal had been laid upon the fire, it was entirely consumed in the flame. The fire was to be kept going all night so that every bit of the sacrifice might be reduced to ashes. It was only then that the ashes might be taken from the altar by a priest wearing linen garments and placed beside the altar. Then the priest, after changing his garments, took the ashes to a clean place outside the camp. The ashes indicated that the perfect offering was fully accomplished and acceptable to God.

Note that in this sacrifice (in contrast to the sin offering), the priests stood around watching the work of the fire. They had sprinkled the blood on the altar and arranged the pieces of the sacrifice, but that ended their participation. There was nothing for the priests to eat. This offering was exclusively for God.

We, as believer-priests, should rejoice in the fact that Christ was the perfect sacrifice that pleased God and has been provided for us.

Again in contrast, all of the burnt offering was burned on the altar, while part of the sin offering was burned outside the camp. The sin offering had sin placed on it and was therefore not fit for burning within the camp. This fact sets the two offerings apart. Further, C. H. Mackintosh, in his invaluable *Notes on the Book of Leviticus* points out the following:

> . . . the Hebrew word which is rendered "burn" in the case of the burnt-offering is wholly different from that which is used in the sin-offering. . . . The word used in the burnt-offering signifies "incense," or to "burn incense," and occurs in the following passages, in some one or other of its various inflections: Lev. vi. 15—"And all the *frankincense,* . . . and shall *burn* it upon the altar; Deut. xxxiii. 10—"They shall put *incense* before Thee, and whole *burnt* sacrifice upon Thine altar;" Exod. xxx. 1—"And thou shalt make an altar to *burn incense* upon;". . . .
>
> The Hebrew word which is rendered "burn" in connection with the sin-offering, signifies to burn in general, and occurs in the following passages: Gen. xi. 3—"Let us make brick, and *burn* them thoroughly." . . . 2 Chron. xvi. 14—"And they made a very great *burning* for him."[2]

How wonderful that the Holy Spirit should make such a distinction in describing the burnt offering. This offering symbolized the Son of God giving Himself in love to the fulfilling of the Father's will. We read, "It is a burnt offering, an offering by fire of a soothing aroma to the Lord." (Lev. 1:17). The sacred writer used this expression to show God's approval of the sacrifice.

The Grain Offering—Leviticus 2:1–16; 6:14–18

The grain offering brings before us a ceremony of quite a different nature. There is no animal involved, no laying on of hands, no sprinkling of blood. This was an offering of worship or fellowship, and it stands in sharp contrast to the burnt offering. This offering depicts our Lord in His life (not His death) as He walked among men.

The offerer brought an unspecified quantity of fine flour, poured oil upon it, and placed frankincense on the whole. The priest received the offering before the altar, took from it a handful of the flour and oil and, in addition, took all of the frankincense. This handful of flour—a memorial portion—was offered up on the fire of the altar to produce a soothing aroma to God.

The fine flour (representing our Lord in his humanity) was produced by threshing the grain, grinding it in a mortar and pestle, and sifting it until it could be pronounced fine. The flour did not contain one coarse grain. Jesus never had to retrace a step. He never recalled a word. In contrast, as recorded in Num 20:7–11, Moses lost his temper and struck the rock to bring forth water when God had told him to speak to the rock. Peter, too, was known for his rash statements, coupled with cowardice. Paul had regrets initially about statements that he made in his first letter to the Corinthians (see 2 Cor. 7:8).

The oil was both mixed with the flour and poured on the

cooked cakes or wafers. In this we see Jesus, conceived by the Holy Spirit in Mary's womb (a mixing with sinful humanity) and anointed by the Holy Spirit for His ministry at the time of His baptism by John the Baptist (see Matt. 3:16). Peter, in the house of Cornelius, reminded the assembled group that God had anointed Jesus "with the Holy Spirit and with power" for going about and doing good (Acts 10:38). Our Lord was both the Son of Man and the Son of God.

The priest took only a handful of the flour and oil but *all* of the frankincense. This lovely fragrance was enhanced by the fire. In our Lord's ministry, He sought only those activities that would bring glory to God, His Father. Every thought, every word, every deed, and every look had only one objective—to glorify God. As His death drew near, He could say, "I glorified Thee on earth, having accomplished the work which Thou hast given Me to do" (John 17:4).

Another ingredient of the grain offering was salt. This common, everyday preservative was important. It preserved the ingredients of the offering and was symbolic of God's covenant with Israel. To the Christian there is the exhortation to let our "speech always be with grace, seasoned, as it were, with salt" (Col. 4:6). Certainly our Lord's words showed the presence of salt as He walked among men. He spoke in tender love to those in need or grief, yet He thundered judgment on those who resisted Him.

One more detail demands our attention. "The remainder of the grain offering belongs to Aaron and his sons" (Lev. 2:3). These sons of Aaron are a type of the Christian as a believer-priest. We, as believer-priests, feed upon the perfections of our Lord. In the previous chapter on the consecration of the priests, we read that they had to be ceremonially holy to serve in the Tabernacle where they ate of the grain offering. Likewise, if we are to feed upon the grain offering—truly worship our Lord—it is necessary that every part of our life—our attitudes, our desires, our associations—have one motive, to glorify Him. The way we speak, where we go, how we conduct our business, maintain our homes, spend our money, and rear our children—all must glorify our Father.

The grain offering could be offered as cakes baked in an oven, or prepared in a pan or on a griddle. In the oven, we see our Lord's hidden suffering for righteousness; the pan or griddle shows us His open or evident sufferings.

A final word. Two things were forbidden in the grain offering, namely, leaven and honey (see Lev. 2:11). Leaven, representing the evil, and honey (natural sweetness), representing passing pleasures of sin, could have no part in the grain offering. Honey was subject to turning sour and thereby introducing corruption which would violate the pure and fine nature of the other ingredients.

The Peace Offering—Leviticus 3:1–17; 7:11–38

In the peace offering we have the third of the worship or communion offerings. Here again, the aspect of sin bearing is not emphasized.

The offerer could bring his offering from the herd or the flock, male or female, but it had to be without defect. He placed his hands on the head of the animal and killed it at the doorway of the Tent of Meeting. Aaron's sons, the priests, would catch some of the blood in a bowl and sprinkle it around on the base of the altar. From the animal was taken the entrails and the fat that is on them, the two kidneys, and the lobe of the liver. If the offering were a lamb, the fat tail was added. These portions were all offered up in smoke on the altar. In Leviticus 7:31–34, we read that the breast and the right thigh were to be for

Aaron and his sons as their due. The balance of the animal was for the offerer who, along with the priests, was to eat of the prepared portions of the offering within the day of the offering and the next. Anything remaining was to be burned.

The peace offering could take on the nature of a thanksgiving, the making of a vow, or a voluntary offering. It truly reflected the attitude of the offerer toward God in the simple act of worship. As it usually followed other offerings, it could provide a fitting climax for all that had gone before. It sometimes bore a subtitle, "the offering of completion."

Note also that in this offering there was something to satisfy the hunger of both the offerer and the priests. Recall that the burnt offering was for God alone, and the grain offering furnished nourishment for the priests, but not the offerer. As the offerer and the priests partook of their portions, they reflected on the peace that had been made, which was the keynote of the entire celebration.

The portions set aside for Aaron and his sons speak of affection (breast) and strength (thigh). The peace that the believer-priest enjoys is indeed precious and complete. The more we reflect on it, the more we realize the depths of love that provided that peace. In John 3:16, there is that little word "so," which portrays the love of God in sending His son to die for us. To attempt to comprehend God's love overwhelms us, and the further we probe, the more the word "so" eludes us. The breast portion is to attempt to satisfy our need for love, and God supplies that need.

The thigh tells us that God possessed the strength to carry out the purposes of His love. In Hebrews 12:2 we read that "Jesus . . . endured the cross." Peter tells us, "Christ has suffered in the flesh" (1 Pet. 4:1).

We, as believer-priests, rejoice in the fact that Christ has "made peace through the blood of His cross" (Col. 1:20). We read that "He came and preached peace to you who were far away and peace to those who were near" (Eph. 2:17). It is as though we had gone into court to answer the charge that we are sinners. We stand before the bench as the judge opens the record. "Yes," he says solemnly, "you are guilty, but here I see that peace has been made. You were at enmity with God, but He has been propitiated. You have been reconciled. The blood of Christ has done it all. There is no claim against you."

> My God is reconciled;
> His pardoning voice I hear;
> He owns me for His child;
> I can no longer fear;
> With confidence I now draw nigh,
> And "Father, Abba Father" cry.

> Charles Wesley

How this fact delights the heart. In the burnt offering, we saw our Lord Jesus as the One who fully accomplished the will of God. In the peace offering, we find the Savior "who loved me, and delivered Himself up for me" (Gal. 2:20).

We now come upon an interesting and significant detail. In Leviticus 7:13, the text reads, "With the sacrifice of his peace offerings for thanksgiving, he shall present his offering with cakes of leavened bread." With leavened bread? Yes. By introducing leaven into the offering, God wishes to teach us His method of dealing with sin in our lives. The teaching rests upon two little words, "in" and "on"—sin "in us" and sin "on us." Before coming to Christ as Savior, we had sin in us received from our earthly parents and also, sin on us—the result of our own doing. We were born with a sinful nature; but when we accepted Christ as our personal Savior, both the sin on us and the sin in us were atoned for. Christ's blood has cleansed from all sin (see 1 John 1:7). "Completely clean" were our Lord's words in John 13:10. However, the sin in us is still there and will break out at the least opportunity. In John's first epistle, he writes that we deceive ourselves, "if we say that we have no sin" (1 John 1:8).

To illustrate the difference between "sin in" and "sin on," let us look at Calvary. There on the hill were three crosses. On the center cross was nailed the Son of God. He had no sin *in* Him, but He had sin *on* Him—the Lamb of God who was made sin for us. Our sins were on Him. The penitent thief had sin *in* him and *on* him. As he turned to Christ and acknowledged Him as his Savior, the sin that was *on* him was placed *on* Christ. The unrepentant thief had sin *in* him, and the sin *on* him remained on him resulting in his condemnation.

The sinful nature that remains in the child of God, even though he is redeemed, will cause him from time to time to sin in word or deed. He lives in a world that is rife with rebellion against God and violates His holy Law. It is so easy to fall in step with the world. Although his sin breaks his fellowship with the Father, it does not change his standing before God! The peace of God (his standing) remains steadfast since Christ made peace through the blood of His cross. However, John tells us, "If we confess our sins, He is faithful and righteous to forgive us our sins and to cleanse us from all unrighteousness" (1 John 1:9). When the believer becomes aware of sin in his life and confesses it, God cleanses him and restores him to fellowship. Confession consists in recognizing the sin for what God calls it, calling it by the same name, and expressing the determination to put it aside. The believer claims the blood of Christ for cleansing, which is faithfully bestowed, and fellowship with God is restored.

Thus, in the peace offering with thanksgiving, the leavened bread is offered, acknowledging the fact that despite the peace with God which has been made sure by Christ, there is the sin in the believer that requires constant alertness and confession if he is to enjoy continuing fellowship with his Heavenly Father.

The Sin Offering—Leviticus 4:1–35; 7:1–7

In Leviticus, we read God's instructions for the sin offering. This was the offering for the anointed priest, the leaders or officers of the tribes, and the common people. In all cases, the offerer identified himself with the sacrifice by the laying on of hands. The priest was instructed to sprinkle the blood seven times before the veil of the Holy Place (God's dwelling place), to put some of the blood on the horns of the altar (the basis of worship), and pour all the remaining blood at the base of the bronze altar (the place of individual approach). The fat, the entrails, the two kidneys, and the lobe of the liver were removed and offered up in smoke on the bronze altar. All of the rest of the sacrifice was taken to a clean place outside the camp and burned with fire.

The sin offering was specifically for the sins of men: "For all have sinned and fall short of the glory of God" (Rom. 3:23). Man is a sinner not because he commits sin; he sins because he is a sinner.

From man's point of view, there are degrees of sin. There is the moral, upright person who is well accepted by society. Often he is the well educated person; the philanthropist, the school teacher, the kind and thoughtful neighbor. Then there is the criminal, the drunkard, and the drug addict. To human beings, the latter is a sinner; the other, not. But God has only one classification—all are sinners. The moral person may have ninety percent righteousness; the person of immorality, thirty percent. But neither can reach one hundred percent—God's requirement, perfection. "Therefore you are to be perfect, as your heavenly Father is perfect" (Matt. 5:48).

God gave His Son to provide the atonement for sin which all have committed, and wonderfully, He includes the sins of which we are not aware and which slip past our consciousness. God has invited us to receive the Lord Jesus as personal Savior, to place our hands (symbolically) upon His head, and know thereby that we are justified and made a child of God. Four times in the fourth chapter of Leviticus the words are used "and he [they] shall be forgiven" (vv. 20,26,31,35). Equally true is God's offer of forgiveness through the shed blood of our Lord Jesus. What assurance can be known by the believer who grasps this truth.

As we compare the sin offering with the burnt offering, we note the following facts. In both, Christ was the offering without defect. Regardless of His work, He was always "holy, innocent, undefiled" (Heb. 7:26). Both sacrifices were killed in the same place and were called most holy. The individual was identified in both sacrifices by the laying on of hands. In the burnt offering, we see Christ accomplishing the will of God to the full; in the sin offering, He meets the depth of our need. In the burnt offering, all of the sacrifice was consumed on the altar; in the sin offering, part of the sacrifice was burned outside the camp.

When the Israelite laid his hands on the head of the sacrificial animal, he symbolically transferred his sins to the animal. The life of the animal was taken, and the Israelite's sins were covered. We claim Christ as our Savior and place our sins on Him. Christ laid down His life for us and our sins are fully atoned for.

The Trespass Offering—Leviticus 5:14–19; 6:1–7

The trespass offering deals with specific sins against God and other human beings. It is interesting to note that all sins are ultimately listed as against God. David sinned when, in order to have Uriah's wife, he commanded that Uriah be placed in the "front line of the fiercest battle" to ensure his death (see 2 Sam. 11:15). However, in Psalm 51:4, David cries, "Against Thee, Thee only, I have sinned, and done what is evil in Thy sight."

The sinning Israelite was instructed to sacrifice a lamb, a kid, two turtle doves or two pigeons in accordance with his ability. In addition, if extortion or robbery was involved, restitution had to be made, plus a twenty percent penalty. Thus, the sinning Israelite was forgiven.

The trespass offering is typical of the Christian's relationship with God, other believers, and non-believers. The old nature of sin is still in us and we cannot sin with impunity. A very subtle offense is the believer's use of his Christian liberty in matters of practice which can confuse and sometimes mislead a new believer or a weaker Christian. Paul encouraged the Ephesians, "Be careful how you walk, not as unwise men, but wise" (Eph. 5:15). We need to maintain a close walk with our Lord, to guard our words and our every relationship with others so that there can be no occasion for regret.

Living before unbelievers, we must be particularly careful to "adorn the doctrine of God our Savior in every respect" (Titus 2:10). The only gospel some may ever read is our daily life.

A life that daily strives to honor and glorify God should ever be our desire. How much we owe to the One who died for us!

> I lay my sins on Jesus,
>   The spotless Lamb of God;

He bears them all and frees us
From the accursed load.

I bring my guilt to Jesus,
To wash my crimson stains
White in His blood most precious
'Til not a spot remains.

I rest my soul on Jesus,
This weary soul of mine;
His right hand me embraces,
I on His breast recline.

I love the Name of Jesus
Immanuel, Christ the Lord;
Like fragrance on the breezes,
His Name abroad is poured.

Horatius Bonar

CHAPTER SIXTEEN

WALKING IN THE WAY

EXODUS 39:32,42–43

"Thus, all the work of the tabernacle of the tent of meeting was completed; and the sons of Israel did according to all that the Lord had commanded Moses; so they did" (Ex. 39:32). We are ready to write "Finis" over this great project that we have studied.

As we look back over the planning, the sculpture, the weaving, the embroidery, the gold smithing, and the silverwork, we stand amazed at the achievements. True it is that Bezalel and Oholiab were filled with skills by the Holy Spirit, but the putting together of this beautiful and complex structure in pastoral society by former slaves was an immense task.

In Exodus 40:17 we read, "Now it came about in the first month of the second year, on the first day of the month, that the tabernacle was erected." One year—twelve brief months—had seen the outpouring of gifts converted into the Tabernacle with its furniture, vessels, and garments of service. This was an incredible feat for the Tabernacle to have been completed in less than a year. (It is estimated that it took the Israelites fifty days to travel from

Egypt to Mount Sinai.) (compare Ex. 19:1 with Num. 33:3).

Not only the artisans' skill, but God's purpose stands out in a study of the Tabernacle. We have followed the sinner's approach to an invitation of God and have seen the vivid way that God portrayed His plan of salvation.

A study of the Old Testament is a study of God's grace. Recall the lesson learned by the despairing couple on the road to Emmaus who felt that their one best hope for the redemption of Israel had been snuffed out on a Roman cross on Calvary. A Stranger joined them and after hearing their heart breaking story, rebuked them as "slow of heart to believe." He began with Moses and "explained to them the things concerning Himself in all the Scriptures" (Luke 24:25–27). "Beginning with Moses" was one of our Lord's methods of teaching. Jesus's reply to His accusers was, "If you believed Moses, you would believe Me; for he wrote of Me" (John 5:46).

As we conclude our study, I want to put into perspective the ultimate purpose for the construction of the Tabernacle. Consider the history of the Chosen People.

In the covenant with Abraham, God had promised that in Abraham's "seed all the nations of the earth shall be blessed, because you have obeyed My voice" (Gen. 22:18). God had, in sovereign grace, singled out a Chaldean herdsman to know Him and to be the channel of His blessing. God had chosen the Israelites that they might be a demonstration and witness to the worship of the one true God. Wherever they went, they were to maintain their distinctiveness from the pagan peoples around them. They were to encourage these people to join them in their worship of Jehovah, making sure that they did not mix pagan practices with the worship of Jehovah. In short, Israel was to have a missionary zeal in making Jehovah known as the one true God.

The Canaanites, among whom Israel was to dwell, were a people whose religion was debased by the use of human sacrifices. In addition, their rites made use of temple prostitutes, male and female, who led them in their worship of fertility gods and the practice of acts of sexual perversion as a part of their normal ceremonies.

In establishing the Tabernacle and the priesthood, God was setting up a visual and dramatic form of religion in which He could show His people that He would come and dwell among them. They were to make no compromise with pagan worship. They were to approach Him only through the shedding of blood in recognition that their sin was heinous in God's sight—so heinous that nothing but the shed blood of an innocent substitute animal could atone for their sin. God reminded Israel that He had chosen them to be a people for His own possession out of all the peoples who are on the face of the earth, not because they were more in number, for they were the fewest of all people, but because He loved them (see Deut. 7:6–8). He came to them in pure grace to provide the way of approach to Himself; there was no obligation on His part to do so. Israel was to carry this message of grace to its pagan neighbors.

Moses spoke to his father-in-law, Hobab, these words: "We are setting out to the place of which the Lord said 'I will give it to you'; come with us and we will do you good, for the Lord has promised good concerning Israel" (Num. 10:29). Such was to be Israel's invitation to the nations they met.

The Tabernacle, with all its furnishings and ceremonies, clearly foreshadowed the One who was to come. The blood of the sacrificial animals was of no avail except as it was to be made effective by the shed blood of our Lord Jesus Christ. He alone could open wide the door of grace for all who would believe—those of Old Testament times as well as those of the Christian era. Hebrews 9:15 reads, "And for this reason He is the mediator of a new covenant, in order that since a death has taken place for the redemption of the transgressions that were committed under the first covenant, those who have been called may receive the promise of the eternal inheritance."

Christ, in His ascension, entered into the Holy Place, Heaven itself, "to appear in the presence of God for us" (Heb. 9:24). Since the earthly Holy Place was a copy of the true heavenly one, we think on the Tabernacle with its gold, silver, embroidery, weaving, and precious stones and conclude that truly, our Heavenly Father, the Creator of the universe, has designed all things beautiful. We are sure that the beauty of Heaven will surpass anything our finite minds can imagine.

> If God has so arrayed a world
>   That quickly passes by,
> Such visions of delight prepared
>   for every human eye;
> What beauty then has God prepared
>   In Heaven for those to see
> Who by His grace shall praise His name
>   For all eternity.
>
> Anonymous

Until then, let those who know Him be encouraged to search the Scriptures to learn more about Him. You will find Him on every page. If you are a stranger to our wonderful Lord, will you not receive Him now by believing God? He says, "But as many as received Him [Jesus], to them He gave the right to become children of God, even to those who believe in His name" (John 1:12).

Then let us go on to learn more of our Lord in all the Scriptures.

More about Jesus would I know
  More of His grace to others show;
More of His saving fullness see,
  More of His love who died for me.

More about Jesus let me learn,
  More of His holy will discern;
Spirit of God, my teacher be,
  Showing the things of Christ to me.

More about Jesus in His Word
  Holding communion with my Lord;
Hearing His voice in every line;
  Making each faithful saying mine.

Eliza E. Hewitt

Notes

CHAPTER ONE

1. C. W. Slemming, *Made According to Pattern*, (Chicago: Moody Press, 1938), p. 13.

2. Paul F. Kiene, *The Tabernacle of God in the Wilderness of Sinai*, (Grand Rapids, Mich.: Zondervan Publishing House, 1977), p. 25.

CHAPTER TWO

1. A large group of people left Egypt. Numbers 1:45,46 states that 600,000 men, besides women and children, made up the group. Some authorities, when counting women and children in addition to this number, plus the mixed multitude that went with them, estimate the total to be about 3,000,000. One authority points out that the word for "thousands" may be translated "clans," and he estimates the crowd to be only around 12,000. My estimate is in between these extremes.

2. James F. Spink, *Types and Shadows of Christ in the Tabernacle*, (New York: Loizeaux Brothers, 1946), pp. 35–36. [The estimates are not sure.]

CHAPTER THREE

1. William R. Newell, *Romans Verse by Verse*, (Chicago: Moody Press, 1938), p. 120.

CHAPTER FOUR
1. Judson Cornwall, *Let Us Draw Near*, (Plainfield, N.J.: Logos International, 1977), pp. 76–79.
2. Ibid, pp. 68–69.

CHAPTER SIX
1. I. M. Haldeman, *The Tabernacle, Priesthood and Offerings*, (Westwood, N.J.: Fleming H. Revell Company, 1925), p. 122.

CHAPTER SEVEN
1. Donald Grey Barnhouse, *Let Me Illustrate*, (Westwood, N.J.: Fleming H. Revell Company, 1967), p. 180.
2. Arthur W. Pink, *Gleanings in Exodus*, (Chicago: Moody Press, 1979), pp. 185–186.

CHAPTER EIGHT
1. Alfred Edersheim, *The Temple, Its Ministries and Services*, (Grand Rapids, Mich.: William B. Eerdmans Publishing Company, 1978), pp. 185–186.

CHAPTER NINE
1. Paul F. Kiene, *The Tabernacle of God in the Wilderness of Sinai*, (Grand Rapids, Mich.: Zondervan Publishing House, 1977), p. 131.
2. C. H. Macintosh, *Notes on Exodus*, (New York: Loizeaux Brothers, Bible Truth Depot, 1879), pp. 336–337.

CHAPTER TEN
1. Judson Cornwall, *Let Us Draw Near*, (Plainfield, N.J.: Logos International, 1977), pp. 98–99.

CHAPTER ELEVEN
1. Donald Grey Barnhouse, *God's River*, (Grand Rapids, Mich.: William B. Eerdmans Publishing Co., 1958), p. 39.

CHAPTER TWELVE
1. Geoffrey Bull, *God Holds the Key*, (London: Hodder and Stoughton, 1959), p. 97.
2. Phillip Keller, *A Shepherd Looks at Psalm 23*, (Minneapolis: World Wide Publications, 1970) p. 57.

CHAPTER THIRTEEN
1. While the account in Leviticus recites two entrances and sprinklings of blood, there is no violation of the "once a year" requirement. It is clear from the text that the two sacrifices and two sprinklings are, in essence, one ceremony thereby maintaining the integrity of one appearing before the mercy seat.

CHAPTER FOURTEEN
1. Arthur W. Pink, *Gleanings in Exodus*, (Chicago: Moody Press, 1979), p. 265.
2. I. M. Haldeman, *The Tabernacle, Priesthood and Offerings*, (Westwood, N.J.: Fleming H. Revell Company, 1925), pp. 300–301.

CHAPTER FIFTEEN
1. Alfred Edersheim, *The Temple, Its Ministry and Services*, (Grand Rapids, Mich.: William B. Eerdmans Publishing Co., reprinted 1978), p. 106.
2. C. H. Mackintosh, *Notes on the Book of Leviticus*, (New York, N.Y.: Loizeaux Brothers, 1880, 1959), p. 23.